D1553891

The Rusyns

CLASSICS OF CARPATHO-RUSYN SCHOLARSHIP

Published under the auspices of the Carpatho-Rusyn Research Center
Patricia A. Krafcik and Paul R. Magocsi, editors

Alexander Bonkáló

THE RUSYNS

Translated by
Ervin Bonkalo

EAST EUROPEAN MONOGRAPHS
Distributed by Columbia University Press, New York
1990

EAST EUROPEAN MONOGRAPHS, NO. CCXCIII

Publication of this volume was in part made possible by a generous grant to the Carpatho-Rusyn Research Center by the Hungarian Research Institute of Canada.

Typesetting and composition courtesy of the Greek Catholic Union of the U.S.A., Beaver, Pennsylvania.

This volume originally appeared in Hungarian under the title *A Rutének (Ruszinok)* and was published by Franklin-Tarsulat (Budapest, 1940).

ISBN 0-88033-190-9
Library of Congress Catalog Card Number 90-81504

Editorial Preface

The series entitled Classics of Carpatho-Rusyn Scholarship is intended to make available in English translation some of the best monographs dealing with Carpatho-Rusyn culture. These monographs will deal with one or more scholarly disciplines: history, language, literature, ethnography, folklore, religion, music and archeology.

The studies included in this series were first published for the most part during the twentieth century and were written in various languages by authors who may have had definite attitudes and preferences regarding the national and political orientations of the indigenous Carpatho-Rusyn population. Such preferences are often revealed in the terminology used to describe Rusyns—Carpatho-Ruthenians, Carpatho-Russians, Carpatho-Ukrainians, Ruthenes, Ruthenians, Rusyns, etc. In keeping with the policy of the Carpatho-Rusyn Research Center, the inhabitants and culture which are the subject of this series will be referred to consistently as Carpatho-Rusyn or Rusyn and the land they inhabit as Carpathian Rus', regardless what term or terms were used in the original work.

With the exception of this effort at terminological consistency, the translations in this series have otherwise not been altered or "improved" in relation to the original works. Whenever the English translation required the addition of a phrase or word, these are set off in brackets. Explanatory notes by the editor to aid the English reader are indicated as such. Incorrect personal or place names, and incomplete bibliographic and footnote references have been corrected or completed wherever possible.

As in other publications of the Carpatho-Rusyn Research Center, place names are rendered according to the official language used in the country where they are presently located; therefore, Slovak in the Slovak republic of Czechoslovakia and Ukrainian in the Transcarpathian oblast of the Ukrainian S.S.R. The international transliteration system has been used to render words and names in the Cyrillic alphabet.

The appearance in this series of scholarly monographs whose authors may favor a particular national (pro-Russian, pro-Rusyn, pro-Ukrainian), political (pro-Czechoslovak, pro-Hungarian, pro-Soviet), or ideological (pro-democratic, pro-Communist, pro-Christian) stance does not in any way reflect the policy or orientation of the Carpatho-Rusyn Research Center. Rather, it is felt that the availability in English of many scholarly studies of varied ideological persuasions is the best way to improve our understanding and appreciation of Carpatho-Rusyn culture.

It was with these principles in mind that we welcomed the offer made by the author's son, Ervin Bonkalo, to make available in English this general study by his father Alexander Bonkáló on Carpatho-Rusyn history and culture. The point of view adopted throughout this book is clearly one which favors the political integrity of the Hungarian Kingdom, whose historic borders had until 1918 reached the crest of the Carpathian mountains and therefore included all of Carpathian Rus'. Moreover, when the original Hungarian-language edition first appeared in 1940, Subcarpathian Rus' had just been reincorporated into Hungary. Clearly, many of the passages in this study are aimed at justifying what was at the time Hungary's newest territorial acquisition. All chapters from the original text are included here with the exception of Chapter 10, a journalist-like survey of the first few months of Hungarian rule in the area after 1939. Because of its chronological immediacy, this chapter was not at all of the same reflective quality found in the rest of the volume and, therefore, warranted deletion.

Admittedly, we found it difficult to accept the strongly anti-Czechoslovak tone in the chapters dealing with recent historical events and with certain of Bonkáló judgements concerning early Rusyn colonization and subsequent cultural developments. On the other hand, the chapters on ethnography, literature, folk poetry, and the church—which make up the bulk of the volume—provide a wealth of invaluable information. Therefore, this volume must be considered a welcome addition to the growing body of publications in English on Carpatho-Rusyns.

Editors

Contents

Translator's Remarks

Alexander Bonkáló wrote *The Rusyns* for Hungarian readers versed in the history of Hungary. Therefore, the translator felt it necessary to add some explanatory remarks to passages that might be obscure for North American readers. These were prepared for the most part by the editors and are indicated by letters, in contrast to Arabic numbers used by Bonkáló for footnotes in the original work. This edition also includes two maps, a biographical sketch of Alexander Bonkáló, and a bibliography of his writings on Rusyns. The reigning dates of monarchs, church hierarchs, and Rusyn activists have also been added in this edition.

I wish to express my appreciation to Professor Paul R. Magocsi of the University of Toronto for making the publication of this translation possible through the Carpatho-Rusyn Research Center, for his editorial notes, and for preparing the maps. The translator has followed the practice of the Carpatho-Rusyn Research Center on place names, although the Hungarian form is added in parentheses the first time the name appears. My special thanks to a life-long friend, Kálmán Kindlovits LLD, of Budapest, who uncovered material for the preparation of Alexander Bonkáló's biography, and to Attila Salga of the Lajos Kossuth University of Debrecen, whose doctoral thesis and publications were an invaluable source in the preparation of Alexander Bonkáló's biography and bibliography.

Finally, I should like to dedicate this translation to Neske, a Hutsul beauty from an earlier time in my life.

Biography of Alexander Bonkáló

Alexander (Sándor) Bonkáló was born on January 22, 1880 in the Subcarpathian town of Rakhiv (Rahó), at the time within the Hungarian Kingdom and today in the Transcarpathian oblast of the Ukrainian S.S.R. Alexander was the oldest son and second of eleven children. On his father's side, the family was Hungarian; on his mother's side, Rusyn. His father, János Bonkáló, a cantor-teacher,[1] was the son of János Bonkáló senior, who had a mill in Synevyr and whose ancestor had come to Subcarpathian Rus' from Transylvania as a *feltser*, or medicine man, with the troops of Rákóczi during the latter's 1703 insurrection against the Habsburgs. His mother, Maria Hadzhega, came from a family of prominent Rusyn priests that included the prolific Subcarpathian church historian Vasyl' Hadzhega (1864-1938) and the theologian and cultural activist Iulii Hadzhega (1879-1945).

The young Alexander attended elementary school in Rakhiv and high school first at the school of the Calasanctius Fathers[2] in Uzhhorod and then in Sighetul Marmaţiei (Máramarossziget). Because his family was poor, he tutored children to earn money for his upkeep. It was the custom in many Greek Catholic families that the oldest son become a priest, so Alexander enrolled in the Greek Catholic Seminary in Uzhhorod where the education was free of charge. Here his talent for languages was noticed. His father, who was a Rusyn at heart, considered it important that his son learn all the Slavic languages, and he knew that this could be best done by total immersion. Therefore, during the summer holidays, Alexander was sent first to neighboring Austrian Galicia to learn Ukrainian and then to Bulgaria. Later he was to go to Poland and finally to the nearby Slovak regions of northern Hungary. Back at the seminary Alexander excelled in Latin and Greek studies, and because of his excellent scholarship he was scheduled to be sent to Rome for ten years of study after ordination. However, six weeks before that ordination was to occur, Alexander changed his mind and left the seminary.

He tried to get a job in Subcarpathian Rus' with his diploma in theology. Although the Greek Catholic elementary schools would have hired him as a teacher, these positions first required the bishop's approval and that approval was withheld. On the other hand, the public schools demanded a teacher's certification, which he did not possess. Having failed in his attempts to secure employment, Alexander went to Budapest, the capital of the Hungarian Kingdom, where he enrolled in the Péter Pázmány University.

His first interest was in Slavic philology, which he studied under the distinguished Hungarian Slavist, Oszkár Asbóth. He also studied Latin and German. In 1906, he obtained his B.A. in Latin, German, and Slavic languages and simultaneously a high school teaching diploma. He taught for a year in Szeged, and then was transferred to Gyöngyös where his intensive work in Slavic philology began. In 1910, he earned his Ph.D. with a thesis entitled "Hungarian words in Subcarpathian Rusyn." Thereafter followed several articles in Slavistic journals published sometimes under the pseudonym O. Rakhovskii. Still other articles he wrote in German. In 1910, he spent four months at the University of Leipzig studying Sanskrit and Russian, and German and French literature. In 1911, he married Edith Kálmán, the daughter of a prominent lawyer in Gyöngyös.

In 1912, Alexander Bonkáló wrote a study of the relationship of Rusyn to the Magyar (Hungarian) language, and the next year he was awarded a prize by the Russian Imperial Academy in St. Petersburg. Subsequently, the university in that same city (now Leningrad) offered him a scholarship, so that beginning in 1913 he spent a year and a half in the Russian Empire, although mostly in the capital of St. Petersburg, he also travelled to Moscow and other larger cities of the tsarist empire. In Russia, he studied Slavic philology with leading scholars like Baudouin de Courtenay, Aleksander A. Shakhmatov, Semen A. Vengerov, and Nikolai F. Iastrebov. He was also invited to participate in Russian literary and intellectual circles, where he met Aleksei L. Petrov, the historian of Subcarpathian Rus', and Vladimir Maiakovskii, the futurist poet. Upon his return to Hungary, Bonkáló's wide ranging comparative book, *The Slavs*, was published in Budapest in 1915.

His scholarly accomplishments and potential led to an appointment in 1917 as an assistant professor of Russian language and literature at the Péter Pázmány University of Budapest. Then within two years came an appointment as full professor. From this new position Bonkáló began in 1919 to organize the first university chair of Rusyn studies.

Bonkáló's scholarly career, however, became caught up in the momentous political events occuring at the time. With the end of World War I fast approaching, the Austro-Hungarian Empire collapsed in October 1918, and early the following month the Hungarians formed a republic under the leadership of Count Mihály Károlyi. The new government was under the influence of the radical sociologist, Oszkár Jászi, who also served as a member of a council composed of scientists, journalists, and foreign affairs ministry employees commissioned to prepare the Hungarian delegation for the upcoming peace treaty talks. Bonkáló was invited by the council to assemble materials regarding the ''Rusyn question.''

Even before the council finished its work, new political changes occurred. Károlyi was forced to resign in early 1919 and a Communist regime under Béla Kun followed. Then in September 1919, the Communists were overthrown and a right-wing government under Admiral Nicholas Horthy took over. It was during the early years of Horthy's regime that this latest Hungarian government accepted, however reluctantly, the provisions of the Treaty of Trianon signed in June 1920, which reduced the size of the Hungarian Kingdom by two-thirds and ratified the new boundaries that saw all Rusyns placed within the new republic of Czechoslovakia.

During these rapid political changes, Bonkáló remained in Budapest where during the academic year 1919-1920 he inaugurated the activity of the newly-established Chair of Rusyn Language and Literature. Under Bonkáló's direction the Chair was to serve as a scholarly resource for information on Rusyns who were to be given a certain degree of cultural and political autonomy within a new postwar Hungary.[3] In that regard, Bonkáló prepared two articles about the Subcarpathian Rusyn language, but they were not published. Moreover, Hungary lost its hold over Rusyn lands, which fell entirely to Czechoslovak and Romanian troops in April 1919.

Nor was Bonkáló's position secure. The Communist regime of Béla Kun regarded him to be a monarchist and refused to authorize publication of his Rusyn studies. For its part, the right-wing regime of Admiral Horthy (which was to remain in power until the end of World War II) thought Bonkáló was a Communist and put pressure on the university to remove him from the Rusyn chair. Even though a special political review committee cleared him of the charges of being a Communist, the attacks continued.

In an attempt to avoid further difficulties, Bonkáló reduced his teaching of Rusyn to two hours and taught Russian literature for only four hours a week. Moreover, in 1922 he published a book, *The History of the Ukrainian Movement*, which because of its own anti-Soviet and therefore pro-Ukrainian sentiment, was pleasing to the Hungarian government.[4] In the end, all this was to no avail. Under the guise of economizing, the chairs of Rusyn and Russian studies (as they became known) were terminated in 1924 and Alexander Bonkáló was prematurely "retired."

Yet even this event did not break his spirit. As the father of three sons, he rounded out his meager pension by teaching Russian correspondence at the Commerical Academy in Budapest and by teaching in a high school of commerce for several years.

Already in 1925, he organized a weekly radio program, on which he spoke about anniversaries in Rusyn and Russian literature. The program lasted for nearly two decades, ending only with the close of World War II. The years 1925 to 1938 were also most fruitful for Bonkáló in the area of translations. The Guthenberg Publishing Company of Budapest launched in 1932 a series entitled "Gems of World Literature." Bound in linen and ornamented with gold, each nation had a different color for its binding. Bonkáló was responsible for Russian literature. His Hungarian translation of Tolstoy's four-volume *War and Peace* appeared in 1933, and it was to be his best work in this genre. As critics pointed out, besides Bonkáló's splendid Hungarian, the translation contained something new. In Tolstoy's original, the conversations of the Russian nobility are in French. Until then, all translators had simply translated these conversations into the language in which the book was published. But Bonkáló left the original conversations in French (providing a Hungarian translation only in the Appendix), reflecting the fact that French was in any case the main foreign language of the educated Hungarian middle class for whom the Guthenberg series was intended. *War and Peace* was such a success that a second edition was printed in 1938. Bonkáló firmly established his name throughout Hungary as a translator of Russian literature. Moreover, the royalties were very good, so that for three summers the family was able to spend its holidays at various Austrian lake resorts.

Initially, Bonkáló wrote all his manuscripts with a pointed steel pen, and in a hand that was very readable. I and my brothers still remember vividly the scratching noise of that pen—the only sound that could be heard from his study. Then, in 1938, he bought a typewriter. Self-taught from books, he typed away with a speed that was the envy of many professional typists! Still, all during this busy period he always found time to help his sons with their school-work. Whether in writing an essay or understanding a speech of Cicero, or in solving problems in chemistry, physics, or differential and integral calculus, he always explained things in a strong yet friendly voice. Remembering this after more than a half of a century, I continue to wonder: how could father do everything?

During all this time, visitors speaking many foreign languages also came to our home, visitors whose names were later to become integral parts of Subcarpathian history. The most outstanding of them was Count Aleksander L. Petrov, who had fled Soviet Russia in 1920 and lived with the Bonkálós in Budapest until 1922, when he was appointed professor at the University of Prague in Czechoslovakia. Petrov's six-foot six-inch broad shouldered and bearded figure was unforgettable. He conversed with father in Russian, with mother in French, and with us children and at the dining table in German. And in his room a candle was always burning under the icon of Maria, his wife whom he had lost during the flight from Russia.

In March 1939, as a result of Hitler's dismembering of Czechoslovakia, Subcarpathian Rus' was returned to Hungary. This was a joyous day for the Hungarian public and, in particular, for Hungarians of Rusyn background like Alexander Bonkáló, who hoped to work once again directly for the welfare of Rusyn culture.

At the end of the war, Bonkáló's university career was renewed, this time under the new postwar pro-Communist Hungarian government. On November 1, 1945, he was appointed professor of Ukrainian language and literature at the University of Budapest. But the appointment was to be short-lived. An unidentified informer accused him of having talked about Soviet literature in a derogatory manner, and this proved to be dangerous at a time when Hungary was becoming a pro-Soviet People's Republic. Therefore, within a year of his appointment, Bonkáló was dismissed, a suspension which lasted from November 1946 until 1950, when, on his 70th birthday he was sent into final retirement.

The real tragedy of Alexander Bonkáló was that he was basically apolitical. As a scholar lacking any real political attachments, he was unfairly accused by every government of Hungary since 1918 of political opposition. Throughout his career, his greatest desire was to preserve the Rusyn culture and language into which he was born. His only political conviction was a firm belief that the survival of the Rusyn people was possible only within the borders of Hungary, a non-Slavic country.

During his first and second "retirements," Alexander Bonkáló consistently showed his interest and love of Rusyn culture. In 1935, he published an illustrated book, *Subcarpathian Literature and Culture*, which was later expanded into the 1940 book, *The Rusyns*, published here for the first time in an English translation.

Bonkáló continued to do scholarly work in Slavic studies and translations of Soviet Russian literature until his last days. He died in Budapest on November 3, 1959, and was survived by three sons. Alexander Bonkalo Jr. (1912-1988) immigrated to Toronto in 1949, where he practised psychiatry and neurology, teaching those subjects for nearly two decades as professor at the University of Toronto. Ervin Bonkalo (b. 1916), the translator of this volume, is a historian and retired university professor living in Canada since 1950, now in Sudbury, Ontario. Tamás Bonkáló (b. 1922) holds the rare degree of "Doctor of Mechanical Sciences" and has remained in Hungary, living in Budapest.

While it is true that during his lifetime Alexander Bonkáló was well known for his translations of Tolstoy, he was generally given little recognition for his scholarly work on Rusyn subjects. He has, however, been remembered after his death. Attila Salga published several studies and completed a Ph.D. thesis at the University of Debrecen (1976) on Bonkáló's life and scholarly career.[5] Moreover, reference works in Slavic and Hungarian studies also refer to Alexander Bonkáló,[6] and in his book on the development of a national identity among the Rusyns (1980), Paul R. Magocsi quotes Bonkáló several times and provides a brief biography of him.[7] Finally, a portrait of Alexander Bonkáló has since the mid-1970s been permanently exhibited in the gallery of scholars at the Ukrainian Research Institute of Harvard University. The present translation of *The Rusyns* will hopefully serve as a lasting testament to Bonkáló's contributions to the history and culture of the Rusyn people.

Ervin Bonkalo

Notes to Biographical Introduction

1. Because in Greek Catholic churches an organ is not used, the cantor occupies the important role of leading the singing "a capella" during the liturgy. The cantor's role in traditional Rusyn society was further enhanced by the fact that he also often served as the village elementary school teacher.

2. The Calasanctius Fathers, a Roman Catholic teaching order founded in Italy during the seventeenth century, maintained before World War II high schools in 33 countries. In all their schools, the emphasis has been on the classics, science, and religion, and as in the Calasanctius Preparatory School still functioning in Buffalo, New York, the student body is usually comprised of the most intellectually gifted.

3. Some efforts were actually made in this regard. With the encouragement of Oszkár Jászi, a specialist on nationality affairs, the government of Károlyi passed a law (December 21, 1918) authorizing the creation of an autonomous Rusyn Land (Ruszka Krajna), which had its own governor and administration that functioned for a few weeks in Mukachevo in early 1919. The Communist regime of Béla Kun allowed a Soviet Rusyn Land with its pro-Soviet governor and administration to continue functioning (actually for 40 days in March and April 1919) until driven out by Czechoslovak troops from the west and the Romanians from the east.

4. Since World War I, the "Ukrainian question" was of importance to Hungary's rulers. As an enemy of the Russian Empire, the Hungarians saw the potential of the Ukrainian movement as a means to weaken tsarist power, and they even published a Hungarian-language journal, *Ukránia* (Budapest, 1916), edited by the Subcarpathian Rusyn Hiiador Stryps'kyi, devoted exclusively to Ukrainian developments in the Russian Empire. After the war, the Ukraine became an important link between Soviet Russia and Béla Kun's Soviet Hungary, and recognizing this fact, the anti-Soviet Horthy regime was interested in knowing about and supporting all anti-Soviet or nationalist Ukrainian endeavors. Hence, the informational services of Alexander Bonkáló were of importance.

5. Among Salga's published studies are: "Adalékok Bonkáló Sándor életéhez és munkásságához," *Acta Academiae Pedagogicae Agriensis,* N.S., XII (Eger, 1974), pp. 201-209; "Bonkáló Sándor és az orosz irodalom," *Acta Academiae Pedagogicae Agriensis,* N.S., XIII (Eger, 1975), pp. 271-281;

"Bonkáló Sándor és a szlávok," *Hevesi szemle,* No. 1 (Eger, 1975), pp. 48-51; and "Oleksandr Bonkalo i rusini," *Nova dumka,* XVIII [73] (Vukovar, Yugoslavia, 1988), pp. 44-46. See also his "Bonkáló Sándor és a keleti szlávok," unpublished Ph.D. thesis, Lajos Kossuth University of Debrecen, 1976, esp. pp. 239-270, which discusses Bonkáló as a Slavic linguist and specialist on the Rusyns.

6. Entries on Sándor Bonkáló are found in the interwar Czech encyclopedia: *Ottův slovník naučný nové doby,* Vol. I (Prague, 1930), p. 678; in the encyclopedia currently in preparation among Ukrainianists in the West: *Encyclopedia of Ukraine,* Vol. I, ed. Volodymyr Kubijovyč (Toronto, 1984), p. 266; and among Carpatho-Rusyn specialists in Czechoslovakia: Olena Rudlovchak's extensive biography of Bonkáló in *Duklia, XXXVII,* 5 (Prešov, 1989), pp. 74-78. Entries on Bonkáló also appeared in two Hungarian literary encyclopedias: *Magyar írók élete és munkai,* Vol. III, ed. Pál Gulyás (Budapest, 1941), pp. 871-873; and *Magyar életrajzi lexikon,* Vol. I, ed. Ágnes Kenyeres (Budapest, 1967), p. 244. The post-World War II Hungarian encyclopedia, *Új magyar lexikon,* 6 vols. (Budapest, 1959-62), has no entry on Bonkáló, while the interwar Hungarian encyclopedia has an entry of a mere one line in the supplement: *Révai nagy lexikon,* Vol. XXI: *kiegészités* (Budapest, 1935), p. 168.

7. Paul Robert Magocsi, *The Shaping of a National Identity: Subcarpathian Rus', 1848-1948* (Cambridge, Mass., 1978), p. 291 (biography) and pp. 70, 111-113, and 119-163 *passim* (discussion of his views and writings).

Works by Alexander Bonkáló
on the Carpatho-Rusyns

1. *A rahói kisorosz nyelvjárás leiró hangtana.* Gyöngyös, 1910.

2. "Hucul népmese," *Nyelvtudomány*, III (Budapest, 1911), pp. 197-201.

3. "Borkut," *Magyar nyelvőr*, XLI (Budapest, 1912), pp. 423-424.

4. "A ruszofil agitáció és a rutén kérdés," *Magyar figyelő*, II, 10 (Budapest, 1912), pp. 87-111.

5. "A görög katholikus magyarság utolsó kálvária utja 1896-1912," *Magyar figyelő*, III, 2 (Budapest, 1913), pp. 291-297.

6. "A sę reflexivum a huczul-kisoroszban," *Nyelvtudomány*, IV (Budapest, 1913), pp. 41-43.

7. "Tagadómondat a magyar-kisorosz nyelvben," *Nyelvtudomány*, IV (Budapest, 1913), pp. 219-221.

8. "Ruténeink irásreformja," *Magyar figyelő*, VI, 11 and 12 (Budapest, 1916), pp. 333-346 and 404-412.

9. [Rakhivs'kyi, O.], *Vyimky yz uhors'ko-rus'koho pys'menstva XVII-XVIII vv.* Budapest: Rus'ko-krayns'kyi respublychnyi sovit, 1919, 24p.

10. *A magyar rutének.* Budapest: Ferdinand Pfeifer, 1920, 79p.

11. "Die ungarländischen Ruthenen," *Ungarische Jahrbücher*, I, 3 and 4 (Berlin, 1921), pp. 215-232 and 313-341.

12. "A rutén kérdés cseh, tót, ukrán és rutén megvilágitásban, 1918-1928," *Külügyi szemle*, VI (Budapest, 1929), pp. 399-409.

13. "Duchnovics, Alekszánder," in *Gutenberg Nagy Lexikona*, Vol. IX. Budapest, 1931, p. 290.

14. "Duliskovics, Joan," in *Gutenberg Nagy Lexikon*, Vol. IX. Budapest, 1931, p. 303.

15. "Petrov történeti könyvei a magyar ruténekről," *Külügyi szemle*, IX, 3 (Budapest, 1932), pp. 336-338.

16. "Magyar emlékek a rutén irodalomban," in *Emlékkönyv Balassa Józsefnek.* Budapest, 1934, pp. 42-45.

17. *A kárpátalji rutén irodalom és művelődés.* Felvidéki tudományos társaság kiadványai, 1 sor., No. 2. Pécs, 1935, 79p.

18. "Czambel és a rutének," in Lajos Steiner, ed. *Czambel emlékkönyv.* Pécs: Felvidéki tudományos társaság, 1937, pp. 138-145.

19. "Hazajöttek ruténeink," *Katholikus szemle*, LIII (Budapest, 1939), pp. 288-292.
20. "Kárpátorosz, nagyorosz, orosz, ruszin, rutén, uhrorusz, ukrán," *Láthatár*, VII, 7 (Budapest, 1939), pp. 292-295.
21. "Ruténeink," *Tükör*, VIII (Budapest, 1940), pp. 371-373.
22. *A Rutének (Ruszinok)*. Budapest: Franklin-Társulat, 1940, 184p.
23. "Rus'kyi lyteraturnŷi iazŷk—A ruszin irodalmi nyelv," *Zoria-Hajnal*, I, 1-2 (Uzhhorod, 1941), pp. 54-71.

The Rusyns

Foreword

This review of the people of Rákóczi,[a] the Rusyns of Subcarpathian Rus', is presented here as a kind of summary of a lifetime of research and writing.

After a co-existence spanning several hundred years, the Rusyns were torn away from Hungary by the imposed Treaty of Trianon signed in 1920. In 1939, after twenty years, they were brought back to Hungary through mutual agreement by our armed forces.

For the Rusyns it was a disturbing twenty years under Czech rule. Day after day Czechs, Russians, and Ukrainians whispered in Rusyn ears a tale of Hungarian oppression which was supposed to have lasted a thousand years. Growing up in the schools of the Czechoslovak republic, the Rusyns believed these tales so that the twenty years of agitation have left a mark on their souls.

Before World War I, the Rusyns did not have nationalist ambitions. Nationalism is generally embedded into the mind of the masses by the educated class. Yet the Rusyns did not have a Slavic-minded middle class. Their sons were not sent to become merchants or tradesmen. Those who obtained a university degree became Hungarian (Magyar) and, furthermore, forgot what little Rusyn language they had spoken in their childhood.

Only after occupying Subcarpathian Rus' did the Czechoslovak government, with the help of Russian and Ukrainian émigrés, begin to make Slavs out of the Rusyns. The school room, the stage, the Orthodox church, and the press cast a shadow over Hungarian customs and Hungarian connections through parades, public meetings, and

---

a. The people of Rákóczi refers to the traditional description of Rusyns in Hungarian literature as the *gens fidelissima,* the faithful people, in reference to their loyalty to Prince Ferenc Rákóczi during his rebellion against Habsburg rule at the outset of the eighteenth century. See below pp. 22-25.

1

amateur dramatic performances. A segment of the Rusyns did undergo a transformation, and gradually ideas of nationalism and a desire to become an independent nation arose among them.

We [Hungarians] should not continue to view the Rusyns through the illusions of the pre-World War I period. The twenty-year period of Czech rule did leave a definite mark on that Rusyn generation which grew up in the schools of the Czechoslovak republic. Therefore, we are obliged to re-educate them with a loving heart so that the Rusyns may once more appreciate Hungarian ideals. We can love others only if we know them. Let us get acquainted with the Rusyns.

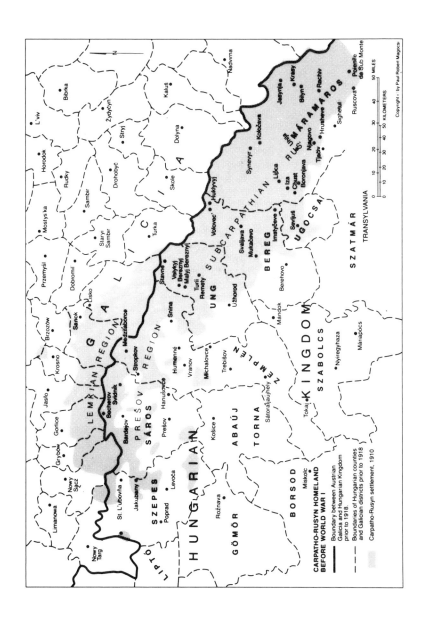

CARPATHO-RUSYN HOMELAND
BEFORE WORLD WAR I

Boundary between Austrian
Galicia and Hungarian Kingdom
prior to 1918.

Boundaries of Hungarian counties
and Galician districts prior to 1918.

Carpatho-Rusyn settlement, 1910

Copyright © by Paul Robert Magocsi

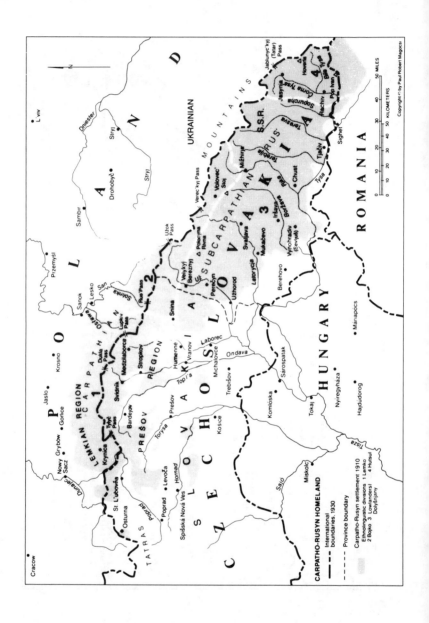

CARPATHO-RUSYN HOMELAND

International
boundaries, 1930

Province boundary

Carpatho-Rusyn settlement 1910
Ethnolinguistic divisions 1 Lemko
2 Bojko 3 Lowlanders/ 4 Hutsul
Dolyšnjany

Copyright © by Paul Robert Magocsi

CHAPTER ONE

The History of Rusyn Colonization

During their 700 years of living on the slopes of the Carpathian forest region, the Rusyns participated in Hungarian history by deeds and by suffering. Throughout this whole period, the Rusyns developed a sense of belonging to the Hungarian homeland. By their activities they proved that they could and would make sacrifices for the homeland. They were grateful to the nation which had given a home and bread to their fugitive and homeless forefathers. They felt with almost a natural instinct that they could live in their mountains only if they could draw upon the grain of the great Hungarian plains. A legend grew out of the strength of this feeling, a legend which proves the Rusyn belief that it is God's will that Magyars and Rusyns belong together:

> Christ was wandering alone on the great highway and met a Rusyn. 'You, Rusyn,' said the Lord, 'come to me tomorrow to work. You will get gold for what you do. If you are industrious you will lay the foundation of your good fortune.'

> The poor Rusyn accepted the offer with great joy for he did not have a penny to his name.

> 'Be at the end of the village tomorrow morning. I will wait for you there,' added the Lord as He continued to walk on.

> As Christ paced along, He met a Magyar. They greeted each other politely. Christ said: 'You, Maygar, would you come to me tomorrow morning to carry out some work? I will pay you well. You will not regret it. If you are at the end of the village early in the morning, I will wait for you there.'

> The Magyar accepted the invitation joyfully because he did not have a penny to his name either.

> 'What kind of work do you want me to do?,' said the Magyar curiously.

'You will learn about it tomorrow morning,' answered the Lord, as He continued to walk slowly.

Night fell. The Rusyn did not close an eye. He worried that if he fell asleep he would not be at the end of the village on time. He took out his boots and repaired them with patches. He asked his wife to cook porridge because he was going to go to work in the morning. He worked on his boots until he finished repairing them at dawn.

The Magyar went home, went to bed, and had a good night's sleep. Jumping out of bed in the morning, he stashed some bread and bacon into his packsack, hung it on his walking stick, put the stick on his shoulder, and rushed to the edge of the village.

Christ was standing near the roadside crucifix.

The Magyar approached him and greeted him politely. 'Here I am Lord. Tell me what kind of work I have to do and what will be my fate?'

'Come with me,' said Christ.

Holding his hand, Christ led him to the edge of the Great Plain and said:

'I give this endless, rich, grain-growing soil to you. Work it well and you will have meat, fish, and bread in abundance.'

'A short time later the Rusyn arrived at the edge of the village. The Lord was waiting for him at the roadside crucifix.

The Rusyn greeted Christ and asked what work would be given to him and what his fate would be.

'You are late poor Rusyn. The good lot was taken by the Magyar.'

'How so?,' inquired the Rusyn indignantly. 'I did not sleep all night in order to be on time.'

The Magyar was smarter than you. He came here first. He took the rich grain-growing soil. But there are the mountains. I give them to you.'

He led him to the hills, where the soil was poor and the yield inferior.

Winter came. Both the Magyar and the Rusyn were unhappy. The Magyar was freezing, for he had no firewood. The Rusyn was starving, for he had no bread. They went to the Lord God to ask for help. The Lord God listened to their grievances and decided thus: 'I have placed you side by side to live together and to help each other. Remember well and follow My command faithfully: you, Magyar, give bread to the Rusyn that he may eat. You, Rusyn, give firewood to the Magyar that he should not suffer cold. Go home and never break my command'.

The Rusyns live in the upland region of the north central or forested Carpathian Mountains, between the Poprad river in the west and the headwaters of the Tysa (Tisza) river in the east. The Rusyn population was made up of several clans or [ethnographic groups]. The varying sizes of these groups can be explained by the circumstances in which they settled and the topographic characteristics of the Carpathians.

The borderline of the area where Rusyns settled starts in the north at the ridge of the Carpathians from the Poprad river to the headwaters of the Chorna Tysa. From there the southern border can be drawn along the southern extent of the county of Máramaros, from the border of Hungary to the Tysa river. The left bank of the river up to Khust (Huszt) is Romanian with the exception of one or two Rusyn villages. The right bank is Rusyn, from Khust to the Zemplén county village of Valaškovce (Pásztorhegy). The Rusyn and the Hungarian border, with a slight interruption, coincided with the borderline formed by the low hills sloping down from the ridge of the Carpathians to the edge of the Great Plains. Rusyns lived in the hills in the area which extends from Khust to Valaškovce southward from the ridge of the Carpathians. Hungarians lived on the plains in this area. Beyond Valaškovce the Slovak and Rusyn borderline was quite entangled. This was a mixed area with scattered Rusyn and Slovak villages. However, only Rusyns lived in the territory closest to the ridge of the Carpathians.

It is not by chance that the Rusyns settled only the region as far as the borderline mentioned above. This line coincided with the inner boundary of Hungary, that is the no-man's land that had been systematically established around the country. During the medieval period, most European countries were separated from each other, not by an imaginary line, but rather by an uninhabited strip so wide that it might have taken days to cross. Hungary had two boundaries: one on the inside, which surrounded the inhabited areas; and another on the outside, which was a conquered or deliberately devastated wilderness. The region dividing the inhabited from uninhabited territories beyond the inner borderline was called the *gyepűelve* in Hungarian, the closest English translation being the no-man's land system.[1] On the other side of the northeast Carpathians, Poland and the Galician principality also had a region dividing the inhabited from uninhabited territory.[2]

The Rusyns lived in our country in an area that once had been the no-man's land separating the counties in the northeast. After the no-man's land system failed in the twelfth century, there was reason for the Rusyns to settle in the Subcarpathian region.

Our [Hungarian] ancestors abandoned the no-man's land system after they were pressed back from the Enns river in the west to the Leitha river. This meant they lost the western no-man's land. Moreover, due to their sad experience during the Mongolo-Tatar invasion of 1241[b] and to the change to the fortified castle system, neither the no-man's land nor the actual no-man's land line offered any safe defence against an enemy attack. The no-man's land itself could hold back the enemy for only a few days, while the no-man's land line (fortifications such as ditches, earthmounds, hedges, wood and stone barricades at the inner borderline) was unable to stop an enemy attack. As a result, our ancestors began to build castles on the mountain tops after the Tatar invasion, and they began to settle the no-man's land areas in order to hold them more easily and to link them to the rest of the country. The hills of the northeast Carpathians were utilized not so much for defence as for economic purposes. Consequently, with the construction of fortified castles, the forests were cleared so that villages were built in forested areas which until that time had been the no-man's land.[3]

This process of settling the uninhabited land in the forested Carpathians began in the thirteenth century following the Tatar invasion. The kings gave large estates in those areas to their faithful followers. Thus, the settlement of the lands became necessary. While there was enough, perhaps even too much land, workers were lacking. Therefore, the landowners imported workers from wherever they could. They found them in particular on the northern and northeastern slopes of the Carpathians in Galicia, Bukovina, and Podolia.

An important fact essential to emphasize is that according to documents the Rusyns had not resided in areas devastated by the Tatars in 1241. The Rusyns were colonists in what was originally uninhabited territory. Documents state that the settlements laid to

---

b. After ravaging several cities in Kievan Rus' during a campaign that began in 1237, the Mongols (together with the Tatar armies under their leadership) captured the capital, Kiev, in December 1240 and then moved westward, entering Hungary in 1241. Of their three entry points into the Hungarian plain, one was directly through forested Subcarpathian Rus'.

ruins by the Tatars lay inside the no-man's land, on the Subcarpathian side of the inner boundary line.

It is true that written sources indicate Rusyns were in Hungary even before the Tatar invasion. However, they had built their homes inside of the no-man's land, not in the Subcarpathian region. We read in the *Chronicle of Anonymous*[4] that when, in the ninth century, the Hungarian chieftain Álmos condescended to receive hostages and presents from the reigning Rus' princes of Suzdal' and Kiev, several Cuman princes requested to be taken along. In this way, many Cuman families came at the time to Pannonia.[c] At the same time, many Rusyns [from Kievan Rus'] joined Álmos, who was about to conquer a new homeland. Their survivors were still living in various parts of Hungary during the lifetime of Anonymous [twelfth century]. The Anonymous Chronicler later stated that Prince Zolta (Zoltán), [Árpád's youngest son], fortified the western border toward Germany and gave orders for a castle to be built by those Rusyns who had come with his grandfather Álmos to Pannonia.[5]

While the Anonymous Chronicler projected the conditions of his own time into the past, his report did have some historical basis. There actually were Rusyns (Rus'), but they were found near the Hungarian-German border at Oroszvár and Oroszfalva [meaning the Rus' castle and Rus' village respectively, today Rusovce] in the county of Moson on the right bank of the Danube below Bratislava (Pozsony). Later documents referred to Oroszvár as Karlburg. Croatians fleeing the Turks settled in that area in the sixteenth century.[6]

Between the eleventh and thirteenth centuries, there was lively contact between Hungary and the reigning Rus' princes of Galicia and Kiev. The contacts began during the reign of Vladimir, grand prince of Kiev (reigned 978-1015). Sons and daughters of the Árpád dynasty[d]

---

c. Before crossing the Carpathians and arriving in the Hungarian plain in the late ninth century, the Magyars inhabited the steppelands north of the Black Sea (present-day southern Ukraine) along the southern boundary of Kievan Rus'. They were driven out of their homeland in the Ukrainian steppe by an invasion of a Turkic people known as the Pechenegs. As a result of their defeat at the hands of the Pechenegs in 889 and their flight westward in search of a new homeland, the Magyars brought with them several minor tribes of Turkic and Ugrian origin described in the Anonymous Chronicles as "Cumani." These Cumans should not be confused with the Cumans (in Hungarian: Kún; in Slavic: Polovtsians) who fled to Hungary during the thirteenth century in the wake of the Tatar invasion.

d. Árpád (ca. 850-907), son of Álmos (ca. 819-895), is traditionally con-

intermarried with sons and daughters of reigning princes at the court of Kiev and with granddukes who were subordinate to Kiev. Our king, András I (reigned 1046-1061), married Anastasia, daughter of Iaroslav the Wise, grand prince of Kiev (reigned 1019-1054). Since it was the custom for princesses to be accompanied by an armed retinue into a foreign country, it is very likely that many of the Rus' (Ruthenus) guards who came to Hungary [with Anastasia] joined the service of the Hungarian king.

Our kings and the Kievan Rus' princes were alternately friend and foe. At times they interfered in each other's internal conflicts. Rus' princes were granted estates in Hungary. Among the freemen, soldiers, and prisoners of war who were settled in various parts of Hungary, there were many Rus' as well. On the other hand, Hungarian settlers are mentioned in Kievan Rus'. When Prince Iurii Dolgorukii (reigned 1120-1157) began in the twelfth century to settle the uninhabited areas of the Suzdal' principality, he invited settlers from many lands, and Bulgars, Mordvinians, Hungarians (vengri) as well as Rus' went there.[7] With regard to Rus' settlements in Hungary, a document known as the *Váradi Regestrum* reports that the castle serfs who belonged to the Kraszna castle and who lived in the village of Ban (before World War I in the county of Szilágy) declared themselves as free Rusyns. A Rusyn named Chedur (i.e., Chevdor, Fedor) even underwent an ordeal of fire to prove that he was a free Rusyn.

There were several military-like settlements in Hungary which were inhabited by free Rusyns. Hungarian documents, various Roman (Latin) relics, many geographical names, and most especially place names with the terms *orosz* in Hungarian, *Rus'/Ruskii* in Slavic, or *Russe/Reusse* in German prove beyond doubt that during the Árpád era Hungary had a Rusyn population in many areas. The documents also prove that the Rusyns did not settle in Hungary at one time, nor in one compact mass, and that since the Rusyn-inhabited areas were found in different sections of Hungary, the Rusyns were amalgamated into the population among whom they lived.

The first dwellers of the village of Nagyoroszi (Greater Rus') in the county of Nógrád were Rus', that is Rusyns invited from Volhynia and Galicia by King Kálmán (reigned 1095-1114) to be made into

---

sidered to be the main tribal leader who led the Magyars across the Carpathians to their new homeland in the Danubian basin. His descendants formed Hungary's ruling dynasty, the Árpáds, who ruled from 907 to 1301.

bodyguards and court doormen *(Rutheni Regia Majestatis)*. They carried out such duties until the time of Nicholas Istvánffy (1538-1615).[8] Archbishop Nicholas Oláh recalls these Rusyns in his work of 1536. He said they were a faithful people who, as commonly known, never committed treason, even as they passed freely in and out of the rooms of the kings and queens.

Later, other nationalities, if they were reliable, were admitted into the bodyguard and doorman staff, and these too received from the king, as did the Rusyns, the title *Rutheni Regia Majestatis*. As in French, the word *suisse* means doorman, because the French nobility and rich Frenchmen imported Swiss doormen, so too the word *Ruthenus* meant not only a nationality, but also an occupation. Consequently, if in Latin documents written in the twelfth to sixteenth centuries we find the word *Ruthenus*, we should not always ascribe to this term Rusyn ethnic origin, because the reference could be to the occupation of the person in question. This is proven by accounts of the king's court during the years 1494-1526, when Rusyns are introduced with names such as Franciscus, Gallus, Oswaldus, and so forth. More precise proof is recorded evidence that on November 14, 1494, *Rutheni Rasci* doormen or guardsmen were on the payroll. *Rasci* refers to Rascian, that is Serbian.

Some Slavic authors argue that the Tisza family is of Rusyn origin, because according to a 1312 document Thyza/Theza Ruthenus was a servant and page of King Károly Róbert (reigned 1308-1342) and later the doorman of his wife. The queen rewarded Thyza for his faithful services with donations of the estates of Örvény, Ludány, and later Borosjenő. The documents state only that the ancestors of the Tisza family served as body guards and doormen. However, the documents say nothing about their origin, so that whether the Tisza family was Rusyn or something else nobody knows. On the other hand, the Rusyns of Nagyoroszi were Rus' by blood and they even kept their eastern Christian religion until the middle of the seventeenth century.[9]

Documents of the Árpád period mention many outstanding Rusyn lords. For instance, Vásoly Rusyn (Ladislaus Ruthenus) received estates in the county of Esztergom, near Párkány, sometime between 1215-1220. Another reference gives information about a most interesting individual who lived during the Árpád period and who was a Rusyn landlord by the name of Maladik. He was captured by the Tatars and was taken with them when they left (1242). There is no record of how Maladik outsmarted the Tatars, but he escaped from captivity and returned to Hungary. While there was no surprise that he had escaped, all were amazed to see the 80 pieces of gold he brought back with him. The documents do not give any indication of how he obtained this great treasure, which meant a great deal to a devastated, looted, poor country. Upon returning from captivity, Maladik heard that the once rich and mighty Hungarian king was poverty stricken and needed money to re-establish the country. So Maladik went to the king and said: "My Lord, my king, accept from me these 30 pieces of gold and use it for the rebuilding of our homeland."

The king appreciated the donation. The rebuilding of the country began. Houses rose over the ruins; the blood-drenched fields were ploughed and the treasury of the king started to fill up again. The king remembered Maladik and called him in order to repay the debt. Rather than accept repayment, Maladik petitioned the king to grant him a hereditary fief, which he received.

At various locations inside the old no-man's land, the scattered Rusyns assimilated with the surrounding people. They became Hungarians, Romanians, or Slovaks, depending on the language spoken in the vicinity where they lived. The surrounding [ethnic] tide swallowed up the small islands of Rusyn settlement. They not only gave up their language, they also altered their religion or rather their rite of worship. For example, the Rusyns of Nagyoroszi in the county of Nógrád still attended mass celebrated according to the Greek rite in 1651, yet by the end of the seventeenth century all followed the Roman Catholic rite; that is, they exchanged the Greek [Byzantine] rite for the Latin.

There was no connection between those Rusyns who had immigrated during the Árpád era and those living in Subcarpathian Rus'. The former disappeared without a trace before the newcomers gained any significance.

The settling of the Rusyns in Subcarpathian Rus'

In 1240-1241, Khan Batu, the reigning prince of the Mongols, put the torch to the barricades from the Veretske Pass to Chynadiieve (Szentmiklós). Near what is today Svaliava (Szolyva), the Mongols killed the border guards and broke into Hungary through the valley of the Latorytsia.

The Mongolo-Tatar invasion destroyed the large landed estates *(dominiums)*, the richest resources of royal power in the entire country, exterminated the population, and annihilated the cultural achievements which had been created through great effort and endurance. The devastated and depopulated country had to be rebuilt. King Béla IV (reigned 1235-1270) invited German settlers, founded towns, and on his own lands gave various privileges to the people who lived there in order to make them able to obtain arms which at that time were an expensive treasure. King Béla IV also donated estates in the northeast Carpathians, within the no-man's land, to his vassals in order to populate the area. This he saw as the best way to protect his domain against attacks coming from the north.

Anna, the daughter of Béla IV, was married to Rostyslav of Chernihiv (d.1263), the reigning prince of Galicia. As a dowry he received Füzér [in Abaúj county] and what was attached to it in nearby Zemplén county. Most likely Rostyslav settled Rus' farmers there. After all, there was great need for workers. Indeed, documents dated from 1254 to 1256 mention Rusyns not far from Füzér, beyond the no-man's land near Subcarpathia northeast from Michalovce (Nagymihály) between the Laborec and Ondava rivers, an area that until then had been totally uninhabited. A 1254 document mentions a *sepultura Ruthenorum*, while a 1256 document talks of a *sepulchrum Ruthenorum quod vulgo dicitur mogula*, i.e., a Rusyn mass-grave or a mound of bodies (*mogula*, in Rusyn: *mohyla*, meaning a burial mound). Some Slavic historians conclude from this thàt by 1254 at least a generation of Rusyns must have settled there. Yet there is a problem: according to the documents, this mass grave was not in a village but was beyond the limits of the completely uninhabited villages of Lesné (Leszna), Čemerné (Csemernye), and Petrovce (Petróc). Since the documents talk of a common mass grave, it is possible that before 1254 there may have been a battle in the vicinity and that the Rusyn soldiers were buried in a mass grave. The kings of the Árpád dynasty and the reigning princes of Galicia had fought many battles. Galician Rusyns attacked Hungary, and in turn Hungarian armies invaded Galicia and Volhynia.

Rusyn settlers were delivered by contractors to the estates after their assignment to the landlords. In the western regions, the contractors who transported Rusyns were called *sholtaz* (in Hungarian: *soltész*; in the eastern regions they were known as *kanaz* (in Hungarian: *kenéz*).[e] As entrepreneurs, the *sholtaz* and the *kanaz* would make an agreement

---

e. *Sholtaz/soltész* derives from the German *Schultheiss*, the elder of a village, and was first mentioned in a document from 1393. *Kanaz/kenez*, from the medieval Latin *kenetus*, derives from the Bulgarian word *knez*, meaning leader, and it was first mentioned as early as 1150.

with a property owner to bring, under certain conditions, serfs to the land. The settlers were to cut down forests, build homes, and establish villages. One condition usually was that the *sholtaz* or *kanaz* would be the chief magistrate of the village. He would collect the taxes and look after the fulfillment of obligations to the landlord. He received additional privileges, such as a larger land allotment or a mill. He was also entitled to receive money or dues from the serf. The *sholtaz* or *kanaz* could sell their offices and the privileges that went with them. As organizers of the villages, in many respects the welfare and future of a given village depended on the talent of the *sholtaz* or *kanaz* to maintain law and order.

The agreements between the *sholtaz* or *kanaz* and the landlord were put in writing. The oldest known extant contract *(literae scultetiales)* is from 1322. It was written for the *sholtaz* of Jakubany (Szepesjakab-falva) in Szepes (Spish) county. The next known document was also from the county of Szepes for the *sholtaz* of Kamienka in 1329. Since the older contracts were written in Latin, I have translated and publish here one from 1579. The introduction and the clause of this is in Latin too.

We, Gáspár Magochy, head of the counties of Torna and Bereg and councilor of his sacred imperial and royal majesty, etc. Let it be known by everybody concerned that we gave Stephen Suk and his younger brother Nicholas Suk, who share bread, the status of *kanaz* to be handed down from son to son, with the same liberties that the other *kanaz* have who belong to the castle of Munkáts [Mukachevo]: to be ready all the time to bear arms. We gave the office to them for another purpose: to establish a village in what is now called the Chasko forest and to name it Felső Mogyorós [today Mykulivtsi], so that the borderlines shall be on the first side, the Visnize creek; on the second side, the new no-man's land in the direction of Mogyorós; on the third side, the road to Pasika; on the fourth side, the Homonnay farm. Yet, they may not take away from another man not even a foot of land. The serfs he receives are exempt from paying taxes for seven years pass, they owe all taxes and dues to the Munkáts castle. To prove this we give our present writing, reinforced with our seal. Dated in the city of Munkáts, the 30th day of July in the year 1579.

Since these and previous writings were followed completely and in all details, we accept and confirm the clauses and details and confirm them with our authority by putting them in writing in order to testify to them. Dated in the city of Munkáts, January, in the year 1613. L.S. Esterházy with his own hand.[10]

The postscript was necessary because the Mukachevo estate had in the interim been transferred to another owner.

We can tell from various documents in what ways the Rusyns came to the originally uninhabited territories. The historian Antal Hodinka established the following pattern:

(1) Settlements came into being from the line of the no-man's land toward the estate borderline in such a way that the oldest settlements were found near the roads leading toward the gates.

(2) The Rusyn colonists did not arrive as a nation or a people, but rather as individual serfs who were convinced to come at various times by a *sholtaz* or *kanaz*. This development is confirmed by the ethnographic characteristics of the Rusyns; namely, there is no unity with regard to their language, physical characteristics, or dress.[11]

The entrepreneurs were not permitted to lure away the serfs of another landlord. Since it was in their own interests to establish the best conditions to which they could convince the people to migrate, they sought simple people. They found such among the Rusyns of Galicia, Volhynia, and Podolia, who lived in very poor conditions, suppressed as they were first by Rus' boyars (nobles) and later by Polish landlords. Neighboring Galicia, in particular, was undergoing a period of civil strife, rioting, and destruction until the fourteenth century when the principality ceased to exist.

The *Galician-Volhynian Chronicle* entry for the year 1227 relates in detail "the countless battles and great deeds, frequent wars and many periods of unrest, frequent revolts and many rebellions." All this was the result of conspiracy and plotting by the "unfaithful" boyars of Galicia. The boyars did not want to obey their lawful reigning princes. They dissented, revolted, fomented disturbances, with the result "that the entire dominion was ravaged. Boyar plundered boyar, peasant the peasant, and one town the other town so that not a single village remained intact, or, as the scriptures say, stone did not remain on stone."[12]

The chronicle testifies how embittered was the struggle between brother and brother, how deep was the hatred between the reigning prince and the "unfaithful boyars" of Galicia and Volhynia. A boyar whose name was Zhiroslav slanderously accused prince Mstislav in the presence of the Galicians that he planned to sell the serfs to his father-in-law for extermination. The innocent Mstislav:

> exposed Zhiroslav and banished him... with the words: 'And now art thou cursed. May you wander groaning and trembling on the earth which had opened her mouth to receive your

brother's blood [from thy hand]'. So did Zhiroslav open his mouth against his master. May he find no shelter in all the districts of Rus' and Hungary and in all other lands. May he roam hungry and in need of wine and oil through all lands. May his household be empty and may there be not a living soul in his village.[13]

While the boyars devastated each other's villages, the poor Rusyn serf had to pay for the ruin. The fate of the Galician peasant became worse after the collapse of the Galician Rus' principality. In 1340, Galician and Volhynian boyars poisoned their last national ruler, [Iurii II, reigned 1323-1340]. The leader of the Rusyn boyars, Dmytro Dedko [took over leadership of the country and then] managed by intrigues to pass the throne of Galicia to Casimir, the Polish king (reigned 1333-1370). The serfs of the Rus' boyar now became serfs of the Polish lord. The Rus' nobility abandoned their serfs, and in order to keep their own privileges and estates they became both Catholic and Polish. This process was repeated in the Balkans as well, where today [i.e., 1940] there is no Bulgarian or Serbian nobility, because in order to keep their estates and to share in the sultan's favors, Bulgar and Serb nobles became Moslems and Turks during the centuries-long Ottoman oppression.

The first Rusyn settlers were led to the lowland plains just inside the old no-man's land line, and only when no more lowland was available were they during the fifteenth to seventeenth centuries settled in the mountainous area (the Verkhovyna). These Rusyn villages began with the *kanaz* contract. If most *kanaz* contracts had not been lost, we could prove the establishment of all Subcarpathian Rusyn villages between the thirteenth and seventeenth centuries, following the failure of the no-man's land system.

The existing *kanaz* contracts are from the county of Bereg, because estates in the Mukachevo and Chynadiieve area kept copies of many *kanaz* documents (in Latin: *litterae kenezioles)*. Organized settlement went on until the middle of the seventeenth century. After 1648, no more *kanaz* documents were issued.

Rusyn settlers continued to pour into the mountainous regions. Even during times when organized settlement was in progress, many Rusyns surreptitiously crossed the Carpathians from Galicia and settled in a small unpopulated valley. Such immigration continued even after the seventeenth century right down to the mid-nineteenth century.

Many folktales recall this voluntary, mostly secret migratory infiltration. The people of Synevyr (Alsószinevér) in the county of Máramaros still tell this tale about the origin of their village:

> A long time ago, there was a dense forest where our village is now. Wild beasts dwelled among the trees and not even nomadic shepherds ventured to go there. From the land of the Liachs [Poland] a man arrived by chance. He came with his wife. He hid in the forest and began to farm. The landlord had not the faintest idea that he had a serf who did not pay taxes and who did not perform any services. A son was born to the couple. He was fed with eggs, poultry, and hare meat. The couple worked all day and ate what they obtained at the same time. They caught fish in the creek, wild animals, or birds in the forest. After four years of farming they had a cow, a few horses, goats, sheep, and a small house and barn was built. For a garden and ploughland a big strip of forest was cut down. Potatoes were planted; rye and oats seeded. They did not lack anything, not even meat. The man hunted; he shot rabbits, deer, and sometimes elk. The wife looked after the house, the spinning and the weaving, and played with her little son. Happily and content lived the Rusyn.

That most villages in the Verkhovyna were founded by volunteer settlers is proven not only by folktales and documents, but also by historical chronicles. The Latin-language chronicle of Huklyvyi (Zúgó) from the eighteenth century, written by the pastor of that village, states that the entire Verkhovynian settlement began in the seventeenth century and consisted of men who liked to hunt and who loved the forests.[14]

After a while the landlord and the treasury became aware of these immigrant Rusyns. For instance, we read in Sigismund Lipcsei's report, written in 1646, that of his thirteen villages only two have a *kanaz* because the other eleven were not planned settlements and originated from quiet, unnoticed immigration.[15] The entire Verkhovyna was populated by such immigrant Rusyns. Sometimes the landlord or the treasury forced them to settle in certain areas. For example, in 1588 Sigismond (Zsigmond) Rákóczi gave a *kanaz* document to his brothers in order to gather the Rusyns who came from Galicia and settle them in Huklyvyi (Zúgó).

The voluntary immigrants had crossed from the northern Galician side of the Carpathian mountains and settled on the southern slopes near the crest. In this manner, the Lemkos who settled in Szepes, Zemplén, and the western half of Ung county [i.e., the Prešov Region], originated from the Galician Lemkos. In eastern Ung and in

Bereg and Máramaros counties, the Boikos too, derived from those in Galicia, while the Hutsuls of the headwaters at the Tysa river had come from the Hutsuls of Galicia and Bukovina.

The northeastern part of Máramaros county received its population last. Here the oldest Hutsul settlment is Rakhiv (Rahó). It very likely had toward the end of the fifteenth century only one or two inhabitants, and in 1600 we find 14 Rusyn serfs. For the land and for the use of the pasture they paid to the treasury one-tenth of their sheep, 14 wildcat pelts, and 1000 trout. They were well off; for example, Mykhail Orosz had six horses, six cows, and 300 head of sheep. Rakhiv and Trebushany (Terebesfejérpatak, today Dilove) were the next places where the Rusyns settled. The first settler of a Hutsul village (the largest in 1639) received in 1658 a tax exemption for twelve years. There was no population in Iasynia (Kőrösmező) in the sixteenth century, for the salt office Coştiui (Rónaszék) reports in 1600 that it was "not feasible for settlement; it is a grassy plain where nobody lives."[16]

The Hutsuls, the inhabitants of the northeast corner of Máramaros county, know themselves that they have not lived very long on the banks of the Tysa river, and this is related in several folktales. In 1912, Vasyl' Marasek of Iasynia told this about the founding of his village:

It was just as I tell it, Sir. I swear it is true. I heard it from my grandfather, let him rest in peace. About 300 years ago not a soul lived where this village stands or around it. Ash forest covered Lazeshchyna, Stebnyi, Lopushanka, and Tyshchora (Chorna Tysa). Within the forest there were clearings covered by rich grass. Knee high grass covered the alpine heights as well. Every spring shepherds from Galicia drove their cattle and sheep here to graze them until the late fall. But once, early in the autumn, wintery weather suddenly descended. High snow covered the hills and valleys, and it turned so cold that a man's breath froze. The shepherds hurriedly gathered their sheep and went home, yet they had to leave the sheep behind, because they could not move in the deep snow. They were left in the valley of the Chorna Tysa. When they returned in the spring to the place they had left the sheep, they were amazed. All the sheep were alive under the ash trees. The poor beasts slipped into the forest litter, ate the ash leaves, and even gained weight and seemed very well in the warm tree litter.
When the farmers in Galicia learned about this, they came into the valley of the Chorna Tysa, built houses, and founded the village of Iasynia.

The remaining Hutsul villages—Kvasy (Tiszaborkút), Bilyn (Bilin), Tysa Bohdan (Tiszabogdány) and others—developed in the seventeenth and eighteenth centuries.

The Rusyns living in Galicia under Polish rule were forced by their social and economic situation to leave their homeland. Emigrating to Subcarpathian Rus' in Hungary they hoped to have a better life than in Galicia. No one forced them to emigrate. The *kanaz* and *sholtaz* had no power over them, and the landlords of Galicia were reluctant to let them go. Therefore, those who wished to leave could only leave in groups during periods of social unrest; otherwise, they came individually, secretly. This explains why it took the *sholtaz* or *kanaz* three to eight years to settle a village.

Among the immigrant Rusyns were some questionable characters. These included deserting soldiers, fugitive serfs, even ordinary criminals fleeing from justice who hid in the Verkhovyna or the headwaters of the Tysa river. Old men of Shyrokyi Luh (Széleslonka) in the county of Máramaros still recalled at the time this book was written [1930's] three vagrants, Pokuba, Selemba, and Dudla, who had founded their village. This explains why sections of the village bear those names. The most doubtful characters were among the Hutsuls of Galicia. Many of them hid and settled in Subcarpathian Rus'.

We know where the Rusyns of Verkhovyna came from, but in Galicia we do not find an analogous group for the lowland or plain-dwelling Rusyns (the *Dolyshniany*). These are the earliest immigrants who settled on the rich soils of the original inner borderline, near the no-man's land. Most likely their original homeland was Podolia or Volhynia.

During the sixteenth and seventeenth centuries, the Rusyns, as the authorities well knew, came to this area later than the Magyars. This is proven by the Latin-language chronicle of Huklyvyi and by birth registers, minutes of canon law procedures, parishes, marginal notes in church books, and family names. Many of the Rusyn immigrants identified themselves by their ancestral village, for example Darivs'kyi (from the Galician village Dariv/Darów), Lypovets'kyi (from Lypovets', Ung county), Tihans'kyi (from Tihany, Abaúj county), Perechyns'kyi (from Perechyn, Ung county).

That the Rusyns came later than the Magyars has been asserted by Austrian and Hungarian authorities as well. This is proven by the request of Geizkofler, the imperial treasurer to the Hungarian nobility. It is also revealed in statements by three officials—Salm, Pappendorf, and Paczot—who were sent in 1570 to the Highlands (Felvidék) by the

Habsburg Emperor Maximilian II (reigned 1564-1576), and who made a report on August 14 of that year in Košice (Kassa), about the same time that reports were being issued by the county chambers of Szepes and Pozsony. The subject arose as part of an argument by Emperor Maximilian II, who demanded from the Hungarian nobility that the Rusyns also should pay them taxes. In the emperor's proposal to the 1572 Diet, he said:

> It is strange and inappropriate that the Magyars, the actual and real possessors of the country should pay decimal taxes, while the Rusyns . . . strangers and vagrants who live the same way from the fruits of the country as the Magyars, should be free as though they would be more noble and better than the Magyars. This is a mockery. Furthermore, when in difficult times the Magyars not only pay taxes but have to suffer and endure other things, they [the Rusyns] should be freed from all burdens like idle onlookers.

Nevertheless, many Rusyns believe and emphasize even today that they are the original inhabitants of Subcarpathian Rus', because they say their ancestors came if not before then certainly with the conquering Magyars. This erroneous belief was first spread by Ioann Bazylovych in his history,[f] in which he also claims that the Subcarpathian Rusyns were Christianized in 867 by the "apostles to the Slavs," Cyril and Methodius. This idea was repeated in the church history of Andrii Baludians'kyi[g] and finally by the schismatic actions of the Eparchy of Mukachevo. The latter made the Rusyns believe that St. Stephen (István), first king of Hungary (reigned 1000-1038), had founded the bishopric of Mukachevo along with other bishoprics. This erroneous statement flattered the vanity of the Rusyns, and it was embedded so deeply in their minds that not even results of the most recent research could completely eradicate it from their common knowledge.

Rusyns for the freedom of Hungary

Until the mid-seventeenth century, the life of Rusyns was peaceful.

---

f. The work in question is by Ioann Bazylovych (Basilovits), *Brevis Notitia Fundationis Theodori Koriathovits olim Ducis de Munkacs, pro Religiosis Ruthenis Ordinis Sancti Basilii Magni, in Monte Csernek ad Munkacs, Anno MCCCLX Factae,* 3 vols. (Košice, 1799-1805).

g. The work in question is by Andrei Baludianskii, *Ystoriia tserkovnaia novaho zavîta,* 3 vols. (Vienna, 1851-52).

They ploughed, seeded, grazed their flocks, and paid their dues to the landlord. They had no cultural demands and were satisfied with their economic situation.

Moreover, the Ottomans did not extend their power to the forested Carpathians.[h] During this time, the Rusyns lived in peace and grew stronger while Hungarian property was devastated by Turkish hordes. Actually, the Ottoman invasion worked to the advantage of the Rusyns because they began to become cultured.

During the Ottoman occupation, Hungary witnessed extensive internal migration. The population of the plains fled to settle in the north and in the northeast. When peace came, many of them returned to their original homes, only to flee again along with another group of refugees in order to seek asylum in the mountains. Therefore, in the sixteenth and seventeenth centuries, a larger number of Magyars fled to territories inhabited by Rusyns.

During those times, many villages which were then Magyars are today Rusyn. In the county of Ung (where today several Rusyn settlements exist), in the seventeenth century we find serfs who had Magyar names. For example according to the 1649 Urbarium from the Mukachevo-Chynadiievo estate, in the 42 Rusyn villages a large number of serfs had Magyar names. Furthermore, even in the northernmost of those villages, such as Volovets' (Volócz) and Trostianytsia (Nádaspatak), there were Magyars. On the other hand, many of the Magyar refugees [who fled north before the Ottomans], including nobles, became Rusyn. This is another reason why there are so many Rusyns with Magyar names, especially among priests and cantor-teachers.

Part of Hungary's population remained on the decimated plains, and we see here, too, that villages were completely re-inhabited, as people of various ethnic origins moved in to fill the places left vacant by departing residents. It was at that time in the area south of the original Magyar-Rusyn linguistic border, that is, the former no-man's land, that Rusyn settlements came into existence.

Rusyns also settled in places where the original Magyar population had died out. For instance, Rusyns from Galicia settled in the north-

---

h. In 1526, the Ottoman Turkish armies annihilated the Hungarian army, killed the king, and for the next century and three-quarters controlled most of the Hungarian Kingdom. Ottoman rule did not extend, however, to the far northern forested regions in the Carpathians (Slovakia, Subcarpathian Rus') nor to Transylvania in the east.

east in the villages abandoned by Magyars. The effect of the contact between Magyars and Rusyns during these migrations is self-evident. The Rusyns learned new concepts [from the Magyars], while the new blood which arrived had a positive effect on their mutual development.

In the mid-seventeenth century, the situation changed as the sound of arms broke the tranquility of Subcarpathian Rus'. The reigning princes of Transylvania led their troops through Subcarpathian Rus' to Poland and, in turn, plundering Polish groups often invaded our country.[i] In 1657, under commander Lubomirski, some 40,000 Polish soldiers looted the counties of Bereg and Máramaros. Actually, in the course of the seventeenth century, invading Polish troops looted Subcarpathian Rus' three times.

However, the greatest suffering was brought to the Rusyns in the eighteenth century by the so-called "Kuruc-Labanc" war.[j] The Habsburg imperial troops and their Labanc supporters made life unbearable for the Rusyns. It is therefore not surprising that the Rusyns, having been tormented by pillage, theft, and arson, expressed understandably enthusiastic joy at the arrival of Prince Ferenc Rákóczi II.[k] They hoped to regain their freedom through him, and for this

---

i. The wars between the Habsburgs and Transylvania were the result of disagreement over the legitimacy of the Hungarian crown. Since the Ottoman invasion of 1526 and the death at that time of the Hungarian king, both the Habsburgs ruling in Vienna and Hungarian princes (mostly Protestant) residing in Transylvania claimed to be the legitimate heirs of the Hungarian crown. By the seventeenth century, Transylvania had become an independent state ruled by the Rákóczi family, which fought against both the Ottomans and the Habsburgs. Rusyn-inhabited Subcarpathia became the boundary between Habsburg and Transylvanian spheres of influence and, therefore, often the scene of bloody battles and the repression of civil disorder.

j. The *kuruc* were originally irregular bands of soldiers and marauders who were discontent with increasing Habsburg authority in Hungary. In 1678, under the leadership of Imre Thököly (1656-1705), the *kuruc* attacked the imperial Austrian army and for the next decade controlled most of northern Hungary in alliance with the Ottoman Turks. After the failure of Thököly and his departure in 1699, the *kuruc* joined the cause of Transylvanian prince Ference Rákóczi II.

The *labanc* comprised Hungarian nobles and their armed forces which supported the Habsburgs and fought bitterly against the *kuruc* rebels.

k. Ferenc Rákóczi II (1676-1735) was prince of Transylvania and leader of a rebellion that began in 1703 against Habsburg rule in Hungary. Imprisoned by the Habsburgs in 1701, Rákóczi sought refuge in Poland, where

reason joined his army by the thousands. Rákóczi later wrote about the event in his memoirs:

> I arrived in Skole [in Polish-ruled Galicia]. When he heard of my coming, good old Petro Kamins'kyi, the archimandrite of the Rusyn monastery [near Mukachevo] who carried me in his arms when I was a child, broke into tears. Not being able to see enough of me, he met me at the border. As soon as the news about me coming spread in the region of Mukachevo, one cannot imagine with what effort and enthusiasm the people rushed to me. . . . These people came to me with wives and children and joined my army not to leave, forever . . . declaring that they wished to live and die with me.[17]

The Rusyn soldiers who joined their leader at the border had only scythes, hoes, and pitchforks for weapons. Only later were they armed by Rákóczi in the hope they could go into combat against the well-equipped Austrian imperial forces. The Rusyn people shared Rákóczi's suffering and did not abandon him when arms were laid down in 1711. The reigning prince had good reason to talk of the Rusyns as the most faithful people—*gens fidelissima*.

Almost everyone in the 161 villages on the estate of Prince Rákóczi II—Chynadiievo and Mukachevo—supplied soldiers, half of whom came voluntarily. Others were recruited to become *kuruc* soldiers, although no one was forced to join. The Rusyn *kuruc* fought in Rákóczi's war of liberation to its end, and they did not return to their villages after arms were laid down in 1711. If they did not fall in battle, they went into exile. Many Rusyn *kuruc* went with their families into neighboring counties, mostly to Ugocsa and Szabolcs. For instance, the annual inventory of the Mukachevo estate has notations after many Rusyn serf names showing that they now lived in Mándok, Pócs (Máriapócs), and Petri (Pócspetri)—all in Szabolcs county—and in other places. The Rusyns who emigrated to the counties of Szabolcs and Hajdú became Magyars in the otherwise Magyar environment.

---

he stayed on the estate of a friend in Galicia, just north of the Carpathians. In June 1703, he heeded the call of a peasant delegation and returned to Hungary by crossing the mountains into Subcarpathian Rus'. His *kuruc* army consisted largely of Magyar Protestant peasants as well as Rusyns who remembered the young prince born and raised at the castle of Mukachevo. His widowed mother had married the *kuruc* leader Thököly when Ferenc was only a few months old, and as a young boy he took part in the defense of the castle against Habsburg imperial troops. The Rákóczi rebellion lasted from 1703 until 1711, when he was forced into exile.

The Rusyn affection for Rákóczi remained even after his death in 1735 as illustrated by the following event. Twenty-seven years after the revolution had been defeated and three years after Rákóczi's death [1738], it was reported to the county government of Szepes that the serfs of the Mukachevo estate had staged an insurrection. When the Rusyn priests urged the faithful to pray for the emperor, who at that time was waging a war against the Turks, the Rusyns grumbled. They said they would not pray for an emperor who burdens them with taxes, custom duties, and other obligations; rather, they would pray for their former lord, Rákóczi, to return to them.

An investigation followed and confirmed Rusyn attitudes. It was disclosed from interrogations and inquiries that the Rusyns really said they would not pray for the emperor; after all, they had a better lot under the Hungarian lords when they paid only 12 florins (florint) a year, while now they had to give 300. The two leaders who incited the insurrection on the Mukachevo estate were each condemned to receive 60 blows with a cane. As a deterrent, the punishment was carried out in the marketplace of Mukachevo in full sight of the crowd.[18]

Nonetheless, the memory of Rákóczi was not beaten by canes from the hearts of the Rusyns, even though it is true that they did not dare to revolt again. Instead, a death-like silence descended upon the Rusyn lands, suppressed as they were by Austro-German landlords.

For a long time the Rusyn people refused to believe that Rákóczi was dead, since they hoped to receive from him an improvement in their lot and to be rescued from the Austrian landlords. For a long time Rákóczi symbolized the redeemer prince. Because he never did return and did not help them, they associated his name with one of their proverbs that reflected a resignation to fate: *Bude, jak Rakotsi priide* (things will be better when Rákóczi will return)—that is, never!

Even at the time this book was written (1939), older Rusyns still told tales about Rákóczi. His picture still hangs in some Rusyn cottages and grandfathers proudly tell their grandchildren: "He loved us, he wanted to help us, but he was exiled, perhaps even killed by the Austrians." In some villages, an old oak tree is shown to visitors, and Rusyns tell how Rákóczi had rested under its shade. Others display a table on which he slept. Before World War I, in the Bereg county village of Pidpolozzia (called in Hungarian Vezérszállás, meaning the Leader's Quarter), a Rusyn farmer proudly pointed out to this author a crate (1½ meters long, 1 meter wide, and 1 meter high), used as a table on which Rákóczi allegedly had slept when he escaped to Poland after being defeated. He allegedly had even carved his initials into the wood. There is hardly a village in the Verkhovyna highlands of Bereg county where, according to tradition, Rákóczi had not passed.

The Rusyns also fought alongside the Magyars in the 1848-1849 war of liberation against the Austrians. However, if in the armies of Rákóczi it was mostly Rusyn farmers who shed their blood, in 1848-1849 it was the Rusyn intelligentsia that rushed to the flags of Kossuth.[1]

The Greek Catholic theology students of the seminary in Uzhhorod, influenced by Petőfi's famous liberty poem,[m] wrote themselves a liberty song to arouse their followers:

Rejoice Hungarians, the battle is won,
Bad dreams of suffering are forever gone!
Your free homeland's sad nights
Filled your suffering soul with sighs,
Awake because the battle is won,
Rejoice Hungarians, the suffering is gone.

You looked at your tyrants—sobbing,
With high hopes gone—at your suffering,
Our complaint, our lament
Brought gloomy days to the motherland.
Awake because the battle is won,
Rejoice Hungarians, the suffering is gone.

Cheers have broken the gloom
Tyrants have met their doom
In cavities of dark graves
To hold despots in their embraces.
Awake Hungarians, the battle is won,
Rejoice Hungarians, the suffering is gone.

Down tyrant into the grave, down to thee,
Our country and nation will be free.
Austria's domination
We swear will never enslave our nation.
Awake because the battle is won,
Rejoice Hungarians, the suffering is gone!

Uzhhorod, 12 May 1849

---

1. Lajos Kossuth (1802-1894), a fiery orator and politician, led the Hungarians in a revolt against Austrian Habsburg rule in 1848-1849.

m. Sándor Petőfi (1822-1849) was a romantic poet whose verses inspired

The theologians of Uzhhorod followed the example of their brother-in-faith, Pál Vasvári,[n] and joined the army to fight for the freedom of Hungary.

Russian spies in Hungary

Toward the end of the nineteenth century, agitation directed from abroad tried to destroy the understanding between Magyars and Rusyns. It is true that official circles in Russia had an eye on the Rusyns long before that time. This was, however, no more than a kind of curiosity and had no serious consequences such as the agitation preceding World War I.

Ivan IV "the Dread" (reigned 1547-1584), ruling prince of Moscow, had adopted the title "Tsar of all the Russians" in 1547. The title actually represented a political program, for the title meant that the tsar was ruler not only of the people living in the Muscovite Empire but also of all "Russians" living in any country (Russians, Belorussians, Ukrainians, Rusyns). Ivan was trying to unite all "Russians" under his sceptre.

In order to achieve this unity, the tsars declared themselves protectors of the Orthodox religion, and under this guise they tried to meddle in the life of Orthodox people of Hungary. Tsar Peter I "the Great" (reigned 1682-1725) first showed much interest in the Rusyns. He promised to support Rákóczi in his efforts to make contact with the Rusyns, with whom Peter the Great had some connections. For example, the mentally-retarded Petro Kamins'kyi, Basilian archimandrite of Mukachevo, was appointed under his patronage bishop of Mukachevo. Tsar Peter hoped that Kamins'kyi would betray the Greek Catholic religion, although the new bishop disappointed him.

Tsar Peter was double dealing. He encouraged Rákóczi but at the same time made an alliance with the Austrian Emperor Leopold (reigned 1685-1705). The cause of this double dealing was the hostile attitude of the Subcarpathian Rusyns toward Peter. Since he could not win them over through ethnic affinity, he and his successors tried to approach them through religion. To fulfill this aim, it was essential to

---

Hungarians in their anti-Habsburg revolution. His most famous poem which became the battle cry of 1848-1849 was "Talpra Magyar" (Arise, Magyar!).

n. Pál Vasvári (1827-1850) was a historian and theoretician of the Kossuth revolution.

be near them all the time, and Peter found a way to achieve this. His ministers Menshikov, Golovkin, Zafirov and others petitioned Rákóczi to grant them vineyards at Hegyalja [in the far south of Zemplén county], where the famous Tokaj vines are grown. When the minister's request was refused, the court of the tsar bought a large estate in Tokaj and nearby Tállya. The vineyard was cultivated by Russian soldiers under the supervision of a Russian general. The Vienna court [the Habsburg emperor was also king of Hungary] accepted the explanation that a true believing tsar can drink only from a vine cultivated by true believers (i.e., the Orthodox). The Vienna court expressed satisfaction with this excuse both during the time of Peter the Great and his successor tsarina Elisabeth (reigned 1741-1762), because they needed the Russian alliance and Russian good will.

However, official circles in both Hungary and Austria were insulted by the presence of a Cossack batallion. They knew that the cultivation of a vineyard by "true believers" was only an excuse to keep tsarist government observers and spies close to the area where Rusyns lived. A priest was sent from Russia to serve liturgy in the Orthodox church of Tokaj for the Russian officers and infantry who were garrisoned in that village and nearby Tállya. The priest was a spy of the Russian court. He observed the Rusyns and did his best to entice them away from the Catholic religion. However, the Catholic church was on the alert, too. As early as 1749 the Hungarian archbishop of Eger reported to royal authorities about Orthodox propaganda among the Greek Catholics being carried out by the priest attached to the tsarist general Vishnievskii. In fact, the activity of the Russian priest did have limited success. In 1760, in the county of Máramaros, and in 1765 at Hajdúböszörmény, he incited the Greek Catholics and got them to return to the Orthodox religion.

Not only the priest, but the tsarist officers and soldiers as well agitated in northern Hungary (Felvidék) and in Subcarpathian Rus'. They were all spies. According to the testimony of documents and contemporary records, there were many soldiers in Tokaj and Tállya. The Orthodox of Tokaj in 1749 asked permission to erect a larger church, because the present one was too small to accommodate the innumerable Russians of Tállya (*obinnumeratam tam Moscovitarium*—there was only room for half of the parishioners).[19] In reality, however, it was the influence of the tsar that was behind the petition of the Orthodox merchants of Tokaj as we learn from a report of [the Hungarian Roman Catholic] archbishop of Eger.

The archbishop notified the Hungarian chancellery that "an extraordinary courier brought him a letter from the court of the tsar in which the tsar asks him for permission to build a church for his soldiers who live in Tokaj." A "ministerial conference" investigated the church building plan and suggested to Maria Theresa, empress of Austria-Hungary (reigned 1740-1780), "to stop the schismatic propaganda of the Russians because it hurts the interests of the ruling church. Since, however, there are friendly relations between the courts of Vienna and St. Petersburg, a compromise is sought. It should be stipulated that the *kalugyer* (Russian monk-priest) should read mass only to the Russians living in Tokaj and should be forbidden to spread [the Orthodox] schism since the archbishop of Eger has already complained."[20]

The Austrian government in Vienna postponed the question of a building permit until the death of tsarina Elisabeth in 1762, and then it asked the Russian government to withdraw its troops from Tokaj and Tállya. The request was not successful. Consequently, the government in Vienna issued an order in 1771, according to which officials of foreign powers living in Hungary would henceforth be put under police surveillance. Not even this scared the Russians away. Some of the troops were called back in 1774, but a new Cossack regiment was sent in their place under the command of Colonel Ravag. Also, a new priest came to Tokaj, Irinei Fal'kovskii, an ambitious and clever monk, with whom the Russian government was very satisfied. Meanwhile, the Austrian government had renewed its [anti-Ottoman] alliance with the Russians [in 1789] and no longer urged the withdrawal of the Russian troops, who actually stayed in Tokaj and Tállya until 1800.

The hundred-year occupation of Russian troops failed to create toward them friendly attitudes among the Rusyns. It did cause, however, much trouble in the religious sphere, because some Rusyns, although officially Greek Catholic, sometimes secretly adhered to the Orthodox religion.

After the departure of the Cossacks, Russian interests were well represented in Buda [the capital of Hungary] in the person of Andrei Samburskii, the court chaplain of the [Russian] grandprincess Aleksandra Pavlovna, the first wife of Archduke Joseph, palatine [1796-1847] of Hungary. The grandduchess had died young [in 1800]. In her memory, the tsar's court built a church at Üröm, a little village northwest of Buda and sent a Russian priest to pray for the repose of the deceased's soul.° The Russian priests lived in Buda and maintained frequent contacts with the Hungarian Slavs who studied at Pest [the city opposite Buda on the left bank of the Danube river]. They also convinced a portion of the Rusyn intelligentsia that the Russian language and literature was their language and literature as well.

One result of this agitation by the priests of Üröm was that many Rusyn writers of the nineteenth century wrote in Russian. Aleksander Dukhnovych, the national poet of the Subcarpathian Rusyns, wrote in 1853 a Rusyn grammar for the Rusyn intelligentsia about whom he was concerned because many had become magyarized. Dukhnovych sent his manuscript to [a fellow Rusyn] Ivan Rakovs'kyi to be published at the Pest University press. Rakovs'kyi, in turn, gave the manuscript to Vasilii Voitkovskii, the Russian priest at Üröm, who completely altered the manuscript and made it into a Russian grammar. In many other ways the Russian priests at Üröm, damaged the interests of the Rusyns. They convinced many talented Rusyns to emigrate to Russia. In this way, Mykhail Baludians'kyi, Ivan Orlai, Petro Lodii, Vasyl' Kukolnyk, Ivan Hutsa-Venelyn, Ivan Deshko and others—all excellent scholars and writers—left the country.[21]

By the end of the nineteenth century, Russian propaganda continued to flourish under the guise of religion. As long as the Rusyn people lived in misery, the Russians were able to lure them with promises of material and spiritual benefits. Such Russian agitation and espionage did not escape the attention of the Hungarian government, although the intrigues were not considered dangerous because the Rusyns more or less disregarded such false prophets. Therefore, the authorities did not consider drastic measures necessary. Only at the turn of the century was there a decision made to cut the wind from the Russian sails. It was decided to raise the intellectual level of Rusyns, to help their economy, and to make reforms that would protect them from harmful propaganda.

The Rusyns in World War I and the detachment of Subcarpathian Rus' from Hungary

During World War I, Rusyns and Hungarians shed their blood side by side. According to the supreme command, there were no incidents in which Rusyn troups exhibited anti-Hungarian attitudes, nor any violations of their oath to king and country.

---

o. The translator visited this chapel in 1938. It is an architectural gem

Until the era of the Czechoslovak occupation, whether for nationalist interests or racial politics, Rusyns never transgressed their
faithfulness to the Hungarian homeland. This was the case even when
the Russian army occupied a part of Subcarpathia for a longer period
of time than necessary and even though Pan-Slavic propaganda was
strong. Of course, there were one or two traitors among them, as
everywhere else.

The memory of great achievements and the suffering experienced
during World War I brought the Rusyn people of Subcarpathia so
close to Hungarians that the official weekly of the Greek Catholic
clergy, the *Görög Katolikus Szemle* (Greek Catholic Observer), protested in its January 20, 1920 issue against the suggestion that Rusyns
are a separate national entity: "The Rusyn people are as organic a part
of the community of Hungary as are the racially pure Magyars. Between the two, the only difference is in language: one part speaks
Hungarian, the other, partially Rusyn. Nationalist desires were never
proclaimed by the Rusyns, neither in the past nor today."

The Rusyns did not abandon their Magyar brothers after the collapse [of Austria-Hungary] in the autumn of 1918. At its formation on
November 9, the Rusyn National Council (Narodna Rada) empha-
sized its adherence to Hungary's territorial entity. When Orest Szabó
(1867-194?), the government minister for Rusyns, began the organization of Rusyn autonomy in Budapest at the request of the Károlyi
regime,[22] the emissary of the Rusyn National Council in Uzhhorod,
Avhustyn Voloshyn (1874-1945), who [two decades] later became
"prime minister of Carpatho-Ukraine," stated at a preliminary conference held on November 29: "Understandably, and out of self-
interest the Rusyn nation does not want to turn away from its
1000-year-old heritage. It does not want to loosen the unity of the
[Hungarian] state in any way either in the areas of religion and education or in constitutional law and public administration, but it wants to
define those desires which promote [the state's] development."[23]

The nationwide Rusyn general rally, held on December 10, 1918,
declared its adherence to the territorial integrity of Hungary. Nevertheless, the Rusyns of Subcarpathia were torn away from Hungary,
contrary to their wish, and incorporated into the newly-formed
Czechoslovak republic. The annexation to Czechoslovakia had been

---

with five small golden domes and a richly carved iconostasis in the interior
which measures only 10 by 12 meters. At that time, each year on the day of the
duchess' death, a liturgy was held that was attended by Russian exiles.

arranged by Galician Ukrainians who emigrated to the United States, and only four Rusyns (more could not be found) living in Hungary discussed it with [the Czech leader] Masaryk, who in turn managed to have the plan accepted by U.S. President Woodrow Wilson.[p]

---

p. Professor Tomáš Masaryk (1850-1937) was a Czech political activist who during World War I lobbied in several capitals of Entente governments, urging them to break up the Austro-Hungarian Empire and to help create a new state of Czechoslovakia. When Rusyn-American immigrant leaders (all of whom were from Hungary, none from Galicia) put their own concerns before United States President Woodrow Wilson, he suggested they contact Masaryk about the possibility of joining Czechoslovakia. At the same time (November 1918) Masaryk was elected in absentia the first president of Czechoslovakia.

CHAPTER TWO

The Rusyns During the Czech Occupation

The peace treaties concluded in the vicinity of Paris[q] tore Subcarpathia away from its mother country [of Hungary] and joined it to Czechoslovakia as an "autonomous Rusyn territory." In its reply to the protesting Hungarian government, the Entente powers stated that the peace treaty with the Czechoslovak republic assured the Rusyns of an autonomy which would make it possible for them to declare their wishes directly and freely. In this regard, the [newly formed] League of Nations was empowered to make helpful decisions.

Therefore, the Rusyns had the right to declare their will after a certain period of time had passed. However, because the Czechoslovak government knew that the Rusyns would demand to be returned to St. Stephen's land of Hungary, it tried to delay that "certain period" in order to gain time to reshape the Rusyn soul and to alienate Rusyns from their Hungarian brothers.

For years the Czechs proclaimed a tale of the thousand-year Hungarian suppression in order to raise distrust and to distract the attention of the Rusyns from the rights secured for them in the peace treaty. However, their plan failed. The Kurtiak-Brodii Autonomist Agricultural Union fought for the rights and the autonomy of the Rusyns consistently and daringly. In fact, the struggle for autonomy began the very day Subcarpathia was annexed to Czechoslovakia.

---

q. The Paris Peace Conference began in January 1919 and resulted in five treaties concluded in 1919-1920 and named after several palaces outside Paris where negotiations were held. The most famous of these was the Treaty of Versailles (June 28, 1919), followed by the Treaty of St. Germain (September 10, 1919), which awarded "Rusyn lands south of the Carpathians" to Czechoslovakia, and the Treaty of Trianon (June 4, 1920), which confirmed the loss of former Hungarian territory to its new neighbors: Czechoslovakia, Romania, Yugoslavia, and Austria.

The American Rusyn National Council (*Narodna Rada*) appointed Gregory Zsatkovich (1886-1967), a Philadelphia lawyer and son of a Rusyn immigrant born and educated in the United States, to carry out during October 1918 negotiations about the fate of the Rusyns with Tomáš Masaryk [the future president of Czechoslovakia]. The executive committee of the American Rusyn National Council acknowledged the agreement with Masaryk, and at a meeting held in Scranton, Pennsylvania on November 12, 1918, declared the annexation of the territory inhabited by the Rusyns in Hungary to the Czechoslovak Republic in exchange for the widest autonomy.

The Treaty of Saint-Germain [September 10, 1919] recognized the annexation of Subcarpathia to Czechoslovakia. In section 10 of the treaty, Czechoslovakia committed itself to the establishment of an autonomous Rusyn province within borders established by the Entente. In appreciation for his services, Zsatkovich was appointed governor of Subcarpathian Rus' (*Podkarpatská Rus*) by the government of Czechoslovakia on April 26, 1920.

Zsatovich was disappointed. Masaryk had not kept any of his promises. Using a variety of pretexts, the Czechoslovak government postponed the drafting of a just Slovak-Rusyn border and the granting of autonomy. Zsatkovich realized that Prague was simply refusing to hear about Rusyn autonomy. Therefore, he resigned on May 16, 1921, and returned to the United States. In an "exposé" to the American government and its president, he made known his inconclusive talks with the Czechs.

Zsatkovich's exposé is an indictment against the perfidious Masaryk and the Czechoslovak government. It disclosed to the world the double-dealing of the Czechs and opened the eyes of the Rusyns. The Rusyn intelligentsia realized that they could not trust the promises of the Czechs. The Rusyns would have within Czechoslovakia only the rights which they could gain by struggling. One memorandum after another was sent [by Rusyns] to Geneva [then headquarters of the League of Nations] which revealed their unsatisfactory conditions. They asked for protection against Czechoslovak suppression, exploitation, and imperialism. However, the League of Nations accepted the Czechoslovak counter-memoranda as truth and filed away the Rusyn complaints. Czechoslovakia had no desire to solve its minority problem, yet it was the Czechs who had urged most forcefully the dismemberment of the Austro-Hungarian monarchy in the name of autonomy for its nationalities.

After Zsatkovich's departure, Ivan Kurtiak (1888-1933), a former teacher in Khust, remained the most enthusiastic fighter for the idea of Rusyn autonomy. His faithful co-workers, Andrei Brodii (1895-1946), Iulii Feldeshi (1875-1947), and Mykhail Demko (1894-1946), supported him with all their power and knowledge. Kurtiak was actually a peasant-politician like the Croatian Stjepan Radić (1871-1928), whom he regarded as his model. According to F. de Gerando,[r] Kurtiak was the embodiment of physical and intellectual power, literally a peoples' leader. His roots were deep in his homeland, and he felt very close to the bread-giving plough and scythe. He was a direct and healthy offspring of the land he loved so much, however poor and wretched it may have been. He was a firm believer in the future of his folk, of the simple, honest, and diligent Rusyn peasants who in their daily prayers, even pray for their enemies.

Kurtiak founded the Autonomous Agricultural Union,[s] which fought courageously for the cultural, economic, and self-governing rights of the Rusyns in the [Czechoslovak national] parliament in Prague. For example, a petition which Kurtiak sent to the presidency of the League of Nations is an extremely important and interesting document, in which he explained how the Czechs violated not only their promise but also section 10 of the Treaty of St. Germain and the appropriate chapter of the [Czechoslovak] constitution.[t] Territorially, the Rusyns were divided into two parts, the document states. About 200,000 Rusyns who dwelt west of the Uzh (Ung) river were thrown into the lap of Slovak nationalists. Moreover, the rights secured for Rusyns in the [international] treaties were being disregarded, and power was in the hands of a Czech vice-governor. The office of the Rusyn governor was an honorary title, and he had no right to pass

---

r. The following description comes from a book that was designed to "reveal" the Communist infiltration of Subcarpathian Rus' under the "leftist" Czechoslovak government. Ferdinand Gerando, *Le complot rouge en Ruthénie* (Paris, 1930).

s. The party was founded in 1920 under the name Subcarpathian Agricultural Union (Podkarpats'kyi Zemledil's'kyi Soiuz) and then changed in 1924 to the Autonomous Agricultural Union (Avtonomnyi Zemledil's'kyi Soiuz). Both were financed by Hungary and supported by the pro-Hungarian Greek Catholic hierarchy.

t. Ivan Kurtyak, *Petition des Ruthénes en Tchécoslovaquie concernant l'autonomie de la Russie subcarpathique* (Uzhhorod, 1928).

orders or decrees. The local Rusyn diet (*soim*) was never convened. The official language was Czech, and eighty to ninety percent of the civil servants were Czechs who did not speak a word of Rusyn. Repression of the [national] spirit was carried on in the schools, while a 40,000 strong official police force and gendarmerie descended on Subcarpathia to strangle any revolutionary activity at its roots and to ruin the economy and the minds of the people. A young Rusyn who had acquired a diploma could not get a position in his own territory, because all positions were filled with Czechs. Only Czechs were employed in important positions.

A classic example of the egostistical, stingy, and imperialistic Czech political thinking was the way the land distribution [from the estates of former Hungarian great landowners] took place. Of the 260,115 acres of land available, the original inhabitants were allotted 19,000 acres. For example in Vuzlove (Bátyú), an area [ethnically] entirely Magyar, hundreds of acres of land were given to Czechs and Moravians, while the indigenous population received only two acres for a cemetery!

Kurtiak's petition was not discussed in the League of Nations. Therefore, the Rusyns decided to stop filling the files of the League of Nations, and instead to take matters into their own hands in order to achieve their rights. For the time being, however, the Czech government was stronger.

The condition of the Rusyns worsened day after day. Famine returned every year. The wonderful Verkhovyna highland plunged into mourning. A dark curse descended upon the green mountains—even the beauty turned into suffering.

> Yammering, cursing, wailing sighs
> Did I hear rumbling there,
> 'Alleluja' ceased to resound
> All the villages only cried.

Gerald Hamilton and Ludwig Renn, emissaries of the International Work-Aid, declared in March 1932, that nowhere did they see such famine and poverty as in Subcarpathia. This included even China where famine and poverty were rampant.

The Czechs did not let in the grain and food collected in Hungary. Due to poverty and the pressures of taxation, the Rusyns staged rebellions in Sevliush (Nagyszőllős), in Perechyn (Perecsény), at Nyzhni Verets'ky (Alsóvereczke) and Turii Remety (Turja Remete).

With ruthless violence the Czech police and army put down all such popular protests.

At Kurtiak's suggestion put forward at his party's congress at Khust on September 18, 1932, a 36-point decision was adopted, the party would struggle in every way for the rights of the Rusyns. However, Kurtiak was unable to continue to struggle to the end for he took ill with symptoms of poisoning and died in the hospital at Sevliush in January 1933.

After Kurtiak's death, Andrei Brodii assumed the leadership of the party. He very energetically demanded autonomy for the Rusyns in order to enable them to look after their own affairs. He knew very well that Subcarpathia complemented economically the Hungarian plains. His people could be happy only if they cooperated with the Magyars and developed with them as they had in the past. Since the Autonomist Union knew very well that if autonomy were granted the Rusyns would decide to return to Hungary, they steadfastly demanded autonomy. To achieve that goal, the Autonomist Union cooperated with the Magyar opposition parties and the Slovak Autonomist (Hlinka) party. Furthermore, they sought cooperation with the Sudeten-German (Henlein) party. The Autonomist Union did not deviate from its orientation even when its leader Andrew Brodii was jailed by the Czechs. The Autonomist Union always looked toward Hungary, particularly to the Hungarian plains where grain was growing for the Rusyns.

The Czechs not only suppressed the Rusyns, they also forced the Magyar, Slovak, and German minorities into a colonial status. Then, when Germany gained strength, it could no longer afford to stand by and watch the suffering of its brothers. It supported with full force the struggle of the Sudeten-German [minority in western Czechoslovakia] which strived to attain territorial autonomy. On May 20, 1938, the Czech government answered the Sudeten Germans and their leader Konrad Henlein with the mobilization of its armed forces. The British government prevented any bloodshed by sending an expert to Prague in an effort to induce the Czechoslovak government to act with restraint. Nonetheless, they were not unaware of the larger situation, and finally the Sudeten Germans had enough of the Czech tactics. After Hitler's September 10, 1938 speech in Nurenberg, the Sudeten Germans demanded annexation to Germany.

Adolf Hitler, the Chancellor of Germany, and Neville Chamberlain, the British Prime Minister, held unsuccessful talks. Following this, at Mussolini's suggestion, the four powers sat down at a conference [in Munich] at the end of September 1938, which decided that the German-inhabited territories of Czechoslovakia would be annexed to Germany and determined that all other nationalities would have the right to autonomy or annexation to the mother land.

After the Munich decision, the Rusyns also wanted to free themselves from Czechoslovakia. Events unfolded with dramatic speed. With the exception of the Communists, all Rusyn parties unified on October 5, 1938. An envoy was dispatched to Prague to press for Subcarpathian autonomy, and when the delaying tactics of the Czech government were discovered, on October 8, at talks participated in by both the Ukrainian- and Russian-oriented parties, Andrei Brodii was elected prime minister. This frightened the Czechs, who now showed leniency in order to gain time. They confirmed the Subcarpathian government and promised the Rusyns independent statehood within the borders of Czechoslovakia.

As soon as Brodii formed his government, preparations were made for a plebiscite. The followers of the Ukrainian orientation and Ukrainian émigrés knew perfectly well that a plebiscite would return Subcarpathia to Hungary, and so they informed Prague. On October 26, the Czech government relieved Brodii of his office and appointed as prime minister Monsignor Avhustyn Voloshyn, the leading figure within the Ukrainian orientation. On October 27, Brodii was arrested for treason and put into the infamous Pankrác jail in Prague where he suffered for four months.

With the help of armed Ukrainians and Czech gendarmes and soldiers, Voloshyn suppressed all manifestations of free will. Modelled after groups in Galicia, he organized a Ukrainian sharpshooter guard (Sich). He also appointed Ukrainian leaders to head the most important offices and to make Ukrainian the official language. He established the Ukrainian National Council, which declared the inhabitants of Subcarpathia to be Ukrainians and the territory to be called the Carpatho-Ukraine. He banned Hungarian-and Russian-language newspapers, put an end to the activity of Rusyn and Hungarian cultural societies, and dissolved the political parties.

On November 2, at a conference held in Vienna, Joachim Ribbentropp and Galeazzo Ciano, German and Italian prime ministers respectively, were chosen to be judges for Hungary and Czechoslovakia and to decide on the new boundaries between Hungary, Subcarpathian Rus', and Slovakia. The Magyars who had inhabited the Highlands (Felvidék) were now returned to the homeland, as the cities of Nové Zámky (Érsekujvár), Komárno

(Komárom), Lučenec (Losonc), Levice (Léva), Jelšava (Jolsva), Rimavská Sobota (Rimaszombat), Rožňava (Rozsnyó), Košice (Kassa), Uzhhorod (Ungvár), Mukachevo (Munkács), and Berehovo (Beregszász) were returned to Hungary. As a result, Magyars who had been prisoners on their ancestoral soil as a result of the imposed Treaty of Trianon now returned to the sceptre of the Holy Hungarian Crown.[u]

The Voloshyn government evacuated Uzhhorod, Berehovo, and Mukachevo, making instead Khust the capital of Carpatho-Ukraine. A constitution was rapidly prepared for the new state, which at the November 22 session of the Czechoslovak parliament became law. According to the constitution, the Rusyn entity was to be an equal partner in a Czecho-Slovak federal state. The three states had a common president and equally shared responsibility for foreign affairs, national defence, and the monetary system. However, the new Czecho-Slovak constitution was just a slip of paper, and despite the protest of Voloshyn, the Czechoslovak government appointed Lev Prchala, a Czech general, as Minister of Home Affairs in the Carpatho-Ukraine with executive power to be in his hands.

Meanwhile, the Ukrainian terror raged furiously. Order, discipline, and the rule of law ceased to exist. Regardless of ethnic and religious difference, the people of Subcarpathia could hardly wait to see the end of the reign of terror staged by the Ukrainian Sich guards. The population of Subcarpathia suffered for five months because the Voloshyn government intended to create a Ukrainian Piedmont[v] based in the forested Carpathians. The Hungarian army could only march in to re-occupy Hungary's ancient patrimony when it became clear that the Carpatho-Ukraine would be unable to fulfill its role as a Ukrainian Piedmont.[w] In any case, a fervent nationalistic spirit was

---

u. The Holy Hungarian Crown or Crown of St. Stephen was given to King Stephen by Pope Sylvester II in the year 1000 A.D. The crown subsequently became the symbol of the unity of the lands in the Danubian Basin within the historic Kingdom of Hungary.

v. The concept of a Piedmont derives from the Italian region of Piemonte, which in the mid-nineteenth century became the territorial basis around which the drive to unify Italy took place. Analogously, in 1938-1939 local Ukrainian-oriented leaders in Subcarpathian Rus' and Ukrainians in neighboring Galicia felt that the Carpatho-Ukraine might with German help become a new "Piedmont" from which to unify the rest of Ukrainian lands (then under Polish, Romanian, and Soviet rule) into an independent state.

w. The reference here to Hungary's reluctance to re-occupy Subcar-

absent among Rusyns. The region was simply not ready, nor were the necessary strategic, economic, and trade foundations present.

Finally, in March 1939, after two decades of bondage, the Hungarian army brought back the Rusyns into the realm of St. Stephen. Just as the Rusyns were happy to be liberated, so too did a kind of enthusiasm touch the whole population of territorially maimed Hungary. The homecoming of the Rusyns was a time for celebration, which fortified faith in the age-long power of Hungary and in the unity of the lands of St. Stephen's Holy Crown.

---

pathian Rus' is related to the fact that Hungary was an ally of Nazi Germany, which for a while supported the idea of a Carpatho-Ukrainian Piedmont as a basis for a future German-dominated Ukrainian state. Only after Germany gave up on the idea of an independent Ukraine did it allow Hungary to press its claims in Subcarpathia.

CHAPTER THREE

Erroneous Teachings about the
Political History of Rusyns

Some Rusyn, Ukrainian, and Russian writers have made great efforts to draw upon the supposed glorious past of the Rusyns and to present heroes from an imaginary shining bygone era. Apart from Hungarian and German historians, the person who took the most determined stand against those story tellers was Aleksei L. Petrov (1859-1932), a historian and professor at the University of St. Petersburg, who was aided by Ivan I. Kholodniak of Moscow University and other Russian scholars.[24]

Petrov revealed that the main pillar of the imaginary political history of the Rusyns—a document dated 1360 in the name of prince Fedir Koriatovych[x]—was actually a forgery composed in the sixteenth century for political reasons and accepted as authentic by Hungarian officials at the end of the seventeenth century. By the outset of the eighteenth century, numerous legends surrounded the name of Koriatovych. Then, at the end of that century, on the basis of various legends, information, and notes originating from unreliable sources (separated often by centuries from each other), and with the aid of uninformed combinations, arbitrary interpretations, and fallacious inventions, a Rusyn political history was developed. Accordingly, the Carpatho-Rusyns, who had settled on the southern slopes of the Carpathians about the same time as the Magyars, possessed as late as the

---

x. Fedir Koriatovych (ca. 1320-1414) was an Orthodox Rus' prince from Podolia, east of the Carpathian Mountains in what is today the Ukrainian S.S.R. When Podolia and other lands of former Kievan Rus' were being annexed by the Grand Duchy of Lithuania in the course of the fourteenth century, Koriatovych quarreled with the new Lithuanian rulers and accepted an invitation by Hungary's King Zsigmond to settle in the northeastern part of the kingdom and help the latter in his own conflict with the Poles. Koriatovych arrived in 1395.

beginning of the eleventh century their own state, Rus'ka Kraina (Rus' Land), that is, the Ukraine. This autonomous Kraina had ruling princes descended from royal blood who lost their privileges only at the end of the fifteenth century. In his commentary on such writings, Petrov wrote:

> Even heroes for this history were found: the 'Rus' voivoda' of 1299, the 'Rus' voivoda Petro Petrovych', and above all, the independent or semi-independent 'by the grace of God, prince of Mukachevo, Fedir Koriatovych'.
>
> Among the educated representatives of an oppressed people, the desire to find consolation, if only in the past, is perfectly natural and intelligible. The Rusyn people, however, should not be afraid of the truth. The political history of the Carpatho-Rusyns is only an illusion, only a mirage. For the present and for the future neither this mirage nor the silhouettes of heroes shining through it can be of any use or have any importance. References to the past of the supposed autonomy of Carpathian Rus' will influence no one. . . . The above mentioned mirage is not only false and useless, it is also harmful. . . because the shadows of the imaginary heroes of the olden times have obscured from researchers the real Carpatho-Rusyn hero—the Carpatho-Rusyn people.
>
> Among this people there were no magnates. The few magnates, like Rostyslav Mykhailovych, Lev Danylovych, and Fedir Koriatovych, were temporary arrivals whose only interests lay outside Hungary. Among this people there was no influential and wealthy nobility. Those individuals who made good disappeared among the Hungarian nobility, while the lesser nobility, military personnel, former castle serfs, and free men as well as the *kanaz* and *sholtaz* were increasingly reduced to the status of serfs. Among the Carpatho-Rusyn people there were no high-ranking prelates in the ruling administration; even the bishop/archmandrite of Mukachevo was a poor man subject to the arbitrary rule of the estate's owners. Among the Carpatho-Rusyn people there was no urban class composed of foreign visitors and endowed with special privileges. As farmer or shepherd, the Carpatho-Rusyn lived in villages; in towns, he merely constituted the unskilled labor force. The Carpatho-Rusyn people consisted of two equally enslaved and equally humbled elements: the peasants and their spiritual leaders, whom the townsmen contemptuously called *bat'ki (batykones)*. It is apparent that such a people in a feudal state could not create any kind of 'history' and that they could only suffer, experience,

and endure on their own the 'history' which occurred in the rest of Hungary.[25]

Petrov goes on to point out that not only the political but also the ecclesiastical history of the Rusyns was invented. This was done by the pious fathers of the Basilian monastery in Mukachevo. In a study on the work of Koriatovych, [the Rusyn historian] Bazylovych[26] claimed the Rusyns had been converted to Christianity by the Apostles to the Slavs, Cyril and Methodius.[y] This erroneous statement of Bazilovych was subsequently adopted by historians of the Rusyns in the nineteenth century (Luchkai, Mészáros, Dulishkovych). Only one more step was needed to proclaim the ancient origin of the bishopric at Mukachevo.

Since the beginning of his own forgeries, Pilgrim, the well-known bishop of Passau, told a tale according to which there were already seven bishoprics of the Eastern-rite in Pannonia during Roman and Gepid times, that is before the Hungarian invasion [896].[27] From this, historians of the Rusyns concluded that one of the seven bishoprics was at Mukachevo. They never even realized that the area called Pannonia [until the nineteenth century] is located downstream, on the right bank of the Danube river, while Subcarpathia is hundreds of kilometers to the east, and on the left bank of the Danube. Nor did they realize that Bidermann's [two-volume history] published already in 1862 and 1867 was based on documents that proved beyond doubt that the tale about the ancestry of the eparchy at Mukachevo cannot be true.[z]

The actual origins of the Mukachevo bishopric reach back only to the fifteenth century. Nevertheless, the 1878 *Schematism* [an annual church almanac] of the Eparchy of Mukachevo published Monsignor Ioann Mondok's essay in which he spoke about a ninth-century foundation for the eparchy. Then, in the 1899 *Schematism*, Antal Hodinka

---

y. Constantine/Cyril (d. 869) and his brother Methodius (d. 884) were Byzantine Greek missionaries who were the first to convert the Slavs, initially the ancestors of the Czechs and Slovaks during their 863 mission to the Moravian Empire. Some writers claim that the brothers visited the Carpathians on their way to Moravia, and that at the very least Mukachevo was one of the original Cyrillo-Methodian dioceses.

z. Hermann Bidermann (1831-1892) was an Austrian historian considered to have written the first professional history of Carpatho-Rusyns: *Die ungarischen Ruthenen ihr Wohngebiet, ihr Erwerb, und ihre Geschichte*, 2 vols. (Innsbruck, 1862-67).

discussed the real history of the eparchy based on valid documents. However, in 1908, the bishop of Mukachevo (Iulii Firtsak) felt it necessary to reprint Mondok's essay because it was more flattering to the interested parties than historical facts.

* * *

To prove the validity of statements regarding the so-called political history of the Rusyns, authors generally cite the following works: (1) the Chronicle of Anonymous; (2) the entry for the year 1031 in the *Chronicle of Hildesheim*; (3) the biography of Konrad, Archbishop of Salzburg; (4) various misunderstood or erroneous data published by Hermann Bidermann and Václav Chaloupecký; (5) a letter of Pope Eugene IV; (6) a document from 1299; (7) tales about a nobleman, Petro Petrovych; and finally, (8) the forged founding document of Fedir Koriatovych.

(1) The Chronicle of Anonymous[aa] mentions in its chapter 10 that Rusyns came to Pannonia with the ruling prince Álmos,[bb] and that their descendants live today (i.e., at the time of Anonymous in the twelfth century) in various parts of Hungary.

Later in chapter 57, Anonymous talks about a ruling prince named Zolta (Zoltán). He had fortified the border with Germany and ordered Rusyns who had come with Álmos [his grandfather] to build a castle. In this way, Rusovce (Oroszvár or Oroszfalu) originated in the county of Moson on the right bank of the Danube below Bratislava (Pozsony).

Anonymous also states what no one doubts—that in the twelfth century, and perhaps even before then, Rusyns lived in various parts of Hungary but not in the forested Carpathians. As proven by documents cited earlier in this book and in other primary sources, they were at Oroszvár, near Krasna (today in the county of Szilágy), in Nagyoroszi (Nógrád county), and in one or two other places as well. These scattered few Rusyn settlements blended in with the Magyar population around them.

---

aa. The famous medieval chronicle by an unknown ("anonymous") author was composed in the twelfth century—long after the events it describes—and is commonly known as the *Gesta Hungarorum*.

bb. According to tradition, Álmos was the Magyar leader who in the second half of the ninth century united the seven Magyar tribes on the eve of their westward move across the Carpathians into the Danubian Basin and Pannonia.

(2) In the *Chronicle of Hildesheim* (*Annales Hildesheimenses*), the entry for the year 1030 reports the presence of troops of the Holy Roman Emperor Konrad (reigned 1024-1039), as well as the emperor himself in Hungary. Then, for the year 1031, it continues: "In this year King Henry, the son of the emperor and ruling prince of Bavaria, and Stephen, the Hungarian king, strengthened their peace with mutual oaths. And during the hunt Emeric, the son of King Stephen who was *dux Ruizorum*, was torn to pieces by a boar, and he died after great suffering."[28] From this report, many writers assume that Emeric was the ruling prince of the Subcarpathian Rusyn marchland (*marchia*).

Yet, according to the findings of Wittenbach, the section of the *Hildesheim Chronicle* for the years 944-1040 is a superficial excerpt drawn from several unknown chronicles; therefore, the entire text should be read with skepticism. For instance, it is known that King Stephen wanted to abdicate in favor of his son Emeric and that the date of coronation was set on September 8, 1031. But Emeric died suddenly on September 2. Because Prince Emeric was a pupil of Bishop Gellért[cc] and someone who had learned to spend his life in prayer and fasting, it is very unlikely that he would go hunting six days before his coronation. Moreover, apart from the *Hildesheim Chronicle* no other source says that he was torn apart by a boar.

The chronicler of Hildesheim honored Emeric with the title *dux Ruizorum*—prince of the Rus'. Prince Emeric's wife was the daughter or sister of Krešimir II (reigned 1000-1030), the Croatian king, and they heard at Hildesheim that he had married a Slavic princess. Even today many people do not know how many Slavic peoples and Slavic languages exist, and still less was known in those days. Since the ruling princes of Kievan Rus' had frequent contact with the West and preferred to marry their daughters to sons of western European kings, they thought in Hildesheim that the wife of Emeric was a Rus' princess who had brought with her as dowry part of a Rus' dukedom. By the way, the Hungarian-Polish chronicle only calls Emeric a prince of the Slavs—*dux Slavoniae*. Finally, there is another reason he could not have been *dux Ruizorum*, because beginning with the coronation of his father Stephen [1000 AD] until the end of the eleventh century, Hungarian princes (*duces*) did not carry the name of their principality (*ducatus*).

---

cc. Bishop St. Gellért was a missionary from Venice who in the year 1000 converted the Magyars to Christianity.

(3) The expression *Marchia Ruthenorum* occurs in the biography of Konrad, archbishop of Salzburg (1106-1147). The biography was written between 1170-1177, long after the death of the archbishop. The author who was a monk, wrote in chapter 18:

> When the archbishop saw that the Hungarians devastated the marchlands (*marchia*), he made peace with their king. . . . After a renewed attack by the Hungarians, I was sent to Hungary as an envoy and I had such great success with the aid of Felician, archbishop of Esztergom, that upon order of the king all prisoners of war were released. This helped increase fear of the archbishop, who at the time was in the [western] *marchia* (i.e., Ostmark/Austria) in the company of some bishops and lords. The news spread through Hungary and both the high-born and the common people were frightened, because it was rumored that the archbishop [of Salzburg] had arrived in the *marchia* to attack Hungary as far as Esztergom, the capital of the kingdom, and to exterminate everything that is living in order to revenge the capturing of his people. When I arrived at Esztergom, I found the archbishop and the population in great excitement. They asked me how I dared to come to the land that my lord wanted to devastate. I did not want to calm them down and denounce the lord's intention of which they were so afraid; therefore, I answered: my lord did not arrive. He decided to wait and see if the prisoners will be returned and the peace kept.
>
> When they heard my reply, they sent envoys to the king who at that time was staying at the *marchia* of the Rusyns (*Marchia Ruthenorum*), and he sent back home all prisoners with their booty.[29]

In 1131, the biographer of archbishop Konrad was in Esztergom, which he thought was the capital [the capital actually was Székesfehérvár], and he did not go into the Rus' *marchia* to see King Béla II (reigned 1131-1141), who had remained at the border of Galicia with his armies. The biographer thought that Hungary had an [eastern] marchland (*marchia*), such as the Ostmark in Austria of the Holy Roman Empire; therefore, he arbitrarily named the eastern borderland of Hungary and Galicia the Rus' marchland (*Marchia Ruthenorum*).

The Latin concept of *marchia* (in German *Mark*: marchland or borderland area) was an institution of the Frankish and later the Holy Roman Empires. A Mark-Graf, that is a custodian count, headed the *marchia* or militarily organized border area. The *marchia* was reinforced by strong fortresses, which also served as focal points for German settlers. The *marchia* had played both a defensive and an offensive role, and its main purpose was the extension of power to neighboring territories of both the Holy Roman Empire and the Pope. After the neighboring areas had been conquered, they were settled by a German population, and a new *marchia* moved farther on.

The *marchia* received its name either from its location (Ostmark: eastern *marchia*), from the time of its foundation (Altmark: old *marchia*; Neumark: new *marchia*), or from the people of the state against which it had been organized. In the time of Charlemagne (reigned as emperor of the West 800-814), the *limes Sorabicus*, i.e. *marchia Sorabicus*, and the *limes* or *marchia Saxonicus* were organized respectively in 805 and 808. The former was the Sorbian marchland and the latter, the Saxon marchland, not because [Lusatian] Sorbians or Saxons dwelled there, but rather because they had been organized *against* the Sorbians and Saxons. Therefore, in the biography of Archbishop Konrad, the *marchia Ruthenorum* does not mean that Rusyns lived there. Rather, it means that it was organized against the Rusyns, or actually against the land of the Rus'—the principality of Galicia-Volhynia.

It is quite possible that during the visit of Konrad's biographer to Esztergom, King Béla II was stationed with his army along the border of Hungary and Galicia, because about that time Boris, the son of Béla's predecessor King Kálmán (reigned 1095-1116) was laying claim to the Hungarian crown.

Hungary had no *marchia* organized according to the Frankish or German model. While the name was not unknown, it was used in the sense of *confinium or fines*, meaning a boundary, or limit. Therefore, the expressions *Alpes Ruthenorum/Alpes Rutheniae* and *porta Russie* mean: "the mountains on the Rus' border" and "the gateway leading to Rus'." They do not mean that Rusyns lived in those mountains or near the gateway (mountain pass). Analogously, in Rus' chronicles, such expressions as "Hungarian mountains," or "the Hungarian gateway" (*gory ugorskiia, vorota ugorskiia*) occur. But these mountains are in the principality of Galicia-Volhynia along the borderline of Hungary, that is, they lead into Hungary.

(4) The otherwise excellent historian, Hermann Bidermann, committed an error which has subsequently been used by other writers to prove that once upon a time there was an autonomous Rusyn state in Subcarpathian Rus'. In the second volume of his history, Bidermann writes: "It is possible that the Rusyn *marchia* [of medieval times] is that boundary line of Upper Hungary which today is indicated by the

expression *kraina*. At present, and depending on the county in which one travels, one may distinguish between the *kraina* of Sáros, Bereg, Ung, or Zemplén. Still, it is quite possible that in ancient times it was an entity headed by a count or voivoda (vajda)."[30]

Bidermann misinterpreted the word *kraina*. He thought it meant "borderline area or boundary," but in fact it originates from the Romanian *craina*. In Subcarpathia, it is mentioned the first time in a document from 1364. South of Mukachevo nine villages were founded and inhabited by Romanians, who formed a separate administrative entity named *kraina/craina* with an elected voivoda at its head. This was the first *kraina* in Hungary. However, the Magyar and Rusyn villages of the province of Bereg did not belong to it. It is very likely that the Romanians had settled there in the fourteenth century. Some moved away, while others amalgamated with the people nearby.

Later, the word *kraina* was used to indicate a *districtus* (district; in Hungarian: *járás*) and *dominium* (estate). For example, in the *urbarium*, i.e., the yearly account of the Drugeth estate in Uzhhorod, the word *kraina* is used to mean estate. All villages of the *kraina* were divided into two parts, with Rusyns in 43 villages and Magyars in 23 villages. In the county of Zemplén, the region of Humenné (Homonna) was called the *kraina* of Humenné, or in Rusyn: *Humenians'ka kraina*. Similarly, the *Kraina Makovitsa* meant the Makovitsa estate. These *kraina* appeared at various times and in various places. The Romanian *craina* means a territory, a county, or a district, and this meaning was adopted in Subcarpathia as well, so that it means an estate or district. Therefore, the word *kraina* is not equivalent to the word *marchia*, and its usage does not prove anything. Moreover, Bidermann mentions it only as a possibility; he does not say *Rus'ka Kraina* means *Marchia Ruthenorum*.

[Another misreading of documents concerns] King Béla III (reigned 1172-1196). He was looking for a French wife, a daughter of a French king, and in that regard his Hungarian envoy produced in Paris an account dated 1184 about the income of the Hungarian king and the Hungarian bishops. The document is known from a fifteenth-century Parisian manuscript that states: "To the archbishopric of Kalocsa belongs. . . the bishop of Bihar, whose seat is Oroszi (*Episcopus Biarch cuius sedes dicitur Orosiensis*)."[31] According to the interpretation of the Czech historian Chaloupecký, in the diocese of Bihar the Rusyn population must have been dense in the twelfth century. During the Czech occupation of Subcarpathia, it was from this mistaken statement (which in the meantime had been withdrawn by

Chaloupecký) that Rusyn writers concluded that the area where Rusyns dwelled extended from Subcarpathia to the southern limit of the province of Bihar. Yet, this was all a misunderstanding. The Latin text: *Episcopus de Biarch, cuius sedes dicitur Orosiensis* means that the seat of the bishop of Bihar is in the village of Oroszi. For example, the bishop of Mukachevo does not live in Mukachevo; he resides in Uzhhorod. Therefore, we could say of him in Latin: *episcopus de Mucachevo cuius sedes dicitur Ushorodiensis*. Moreover, since in Bihar there were two villages by the name Oroszi, the suggestion of [the Hungarian historian] Henrik Marczali may be true: that the name Oroszi is an error in the document and that the correct name of the place is (Várad-) Olaszi.

(5) Elsewhere another Czech historian Lubor Niederle and other Slav writers asserted that in a letter of Pope Eugene IV (reigned 1431-1437), he stated that in 1446 a large number of Rusyns lived in Hungary and Transylvania. It is very likely that there were many Rusyns in Hungary at the time, but not as many as is proven by the letter of Pope Eugene IV. His Latin text reads: *Percepimus quod in regno Hungariae illiusque confiniis et Transylvanis partibus n o n n u l l i Rutheni nunbupati, gens quidem satis populosa et grandis numero, existant* (We heard that in the Hungarian kingdom along its borders and in Transylvania there are also *not many* Rusyns. But this people exists in large numbers).[32] According to the Pope there are many Rusyns, but few (*nonnulli*) live in Hungary and Transylvania.

(6) Bidermann calls Gregory the custodian-count (*Markgraf*) of Rus'ka Kraina, who at the end of the thirteenth century was the lieutenant-governor of Bereg county. In this regard, Katona had published a document with a wrong reading—*Gregorius officialis seu ducis Ruthenorum*—in which he wrote *seu* instead of Lev (Leo). This makes no sense. Therefore, Bidermann omitted *seu*, while others arbitrarily corrected the text to read: *Gregor officialis dux Ruthenorum* ("Gregor, the ruler, prince of the Rusyns"). Yet, the correct text of the 1299 document is: *Nos, Gregorius, comes de Beregh, officialis Lev, ducis Ruthenorum*, which means: "We Gregory, of the county of Bereg, official and representative of Lev, the ruling prince of the Rusyns."[33] Consequently, the Galician Rus' prince was Lev Danylovych (reigned 1264-1301), the ruling prince of Galicia.

The Mukachevo estate was donated many times to foreigners by the kings of Hungary. Konstantiia, the wife of Lev Danylovych, ruling prince of Galicia, was the daughter of Béla IV, king of Hungary (reigned 1235-1270). She brought as a dowry the estate of Mukachevo, but because Lev could not look after it, he appointed Gregory as lieutenant-governor of the county of Bereg. Before then, the estate was owned by the other son-in-law of Béla, Rostyslav Mykhailovych. Then, at the end of the fourteenth century, the estate was given to Fedir Koriatovych, prince of Podolia, by King Zsigmond (Sigismund, reigned 1387-1437), and in the fifteenth century it was given to Branković, the Serbian oligarch. As for the Galician ruler Lev, he died in 1301, after which date Gregory no longer acted as *officialis ducis Ruthenorum*, that is the official of the [Galician] Rus' ruling prince.

(7) After the death in 1301 of Endre III (Andrew), the last of [Hungary's founding] Árpád dynasty, the right to elect a king went back to the Hungarian nation. However, real power was in the hands of oligarchs or mini-rulers of whom Máté Csák of the county of Trencsén; László Kún, the voivoda of Transylvania; and Amadek Aba were the most dangerous. Although in 1308 the Diet of Rákos recognized Károly Róbert (reigned 1308-1342) of the House of Anjou as the only king of Hungary (and Máté Csák acknowledged him too), somewhat later Máté rebelled against his lawful king and began about 1311 to devastate the estates of those who were loyal to the king.

Among those who joined Máté Csák was Petro Petrovych, or Petune (Petheunc, Pethunya, Pethen) of the Aba family, who was the lieutenant-governor of Ung and Zemplén counties. Later, the historian Károly Mészáros invented the following tale about the anti-royal rebellion.

[Before] the rebellion of the Rusyns in the counties of Ung and Zemplén under Petro Petrovych (Péter Pető), . . . the fate of the Hungarian Rusyns was unbearable, not only because they completely lost their political rights just like the other races, but also because they lost the independence of their church—the free practice of their church rites. The only thing remaining was the language of their religion. The free election of their superiors (bishops) was annihilated forever. This extremely painful and unfortunate event for the church of the Hungarian Rusyns and for the nation was perpetuated by the agreement between the Pope and King Károly [Róbert] in 1317, according to which the Pope would receive half the income of vacant episcopal estates. It is natural that this agreement, which hit hard not only the Greek Catholic but also the Roman Catholic priests, created great opposition. The county was flooded with factions (especially those supported by the famous oligarch Máté Csák), which broke away; they found more cause for inner strife and

especially for the unrest of the suppressed churches and of the
Rusyn people. This is revealed especially by the horrible revolt
which broke out among the people in 1320 in the county of Ung,
where Petro Petrovych, the lieutenant-governor of Ung and
Zemplén, made himself leader of the Rusyn-speaking (mostly
Greek Catholic) population in order to avenge fully both himself
and the suppressed Greek Catholic folk. To this end, he
established diplomatic relations with Russia. Some historians
seek the reason for the revolt in the reaction of factional leaders
to the violation of their rights; yet, if we take into consideration
the development and disparate elements of the revolt, we must
confess that they are very one-sided. Because the followers of
Petrovych from the counties of Ung and Zemplén consisted
mainly of Eastern-rite Rusyns, it is certain that if the rebellion
had not been directed at securing their religious interests (and
perhaps too for personal gain), they would not have taken up
arms. Later, the relations of Petrovych with Russia show clearly
that his goal had been the betterment of political and religious
conditions as a whole. A frustrated oligarch would not have con-
tacted such a large empire as the Russian for purely selfish
reasons. However, this move with its daring enterprise was not
successful, and when he received inadequate help both from
Russia and from his people, Petrovych lost interest and was
defeated by Dózsa, the voivoda of Transylvania. The outcome
of this unfortunate initiative caused the rebellious population
great misery both politically and religiously.[34]

Mészáros considered the Roman Catholic Petrovych
(Pető/Petune), who came from the Aba family, to be an Eastern-rite
Rusyn lord. Subsequently, his tale was accepted by some Rusyn
writers (Dulishkovych, Sulynchak, Kondratovych), and what is more,
Stryps'kyi rusynized Pethune's name, making it Petjenko. Hence, this
Hungarian landlord entered latter-day literature with the name Petjenko, and the [Carpatho-Rusyn writer] Vasyl' Grendzha-Dons'kyi
wrote the epic poem *Petro Petrovych* (1937), describing how he osten-
sibly fought for the Eastern rite and his Rusyn people.

Pethune (Petheune/Pethina), whose name was changed to Pet-
jenko/Petrovych, was not a Rusyn. A document from 1255 mentions
his father as *Magister Petrus, dictus Petheunc de genere Aba*, which
means: Master Péter, called Petheune, from the Aba family. A 1263
document cites him as *magister Petrus dictus* Petina, i.e. Master
Péter, called Petina. That he was Roman Catholic is proven by a
document issued by King Károly Róbert in 1312, which mentions that
Master Péter's church in Gálszécs had been ransacked: *ecclesiam*

magistri Petri says the Latin text. It should be noted that only the Roman rite church is called *ecclesia* in the documents, while for all other churches the specific denomination is always indicated.

The Czech scholar Karel Kadlec proved that at the time of Petrovych's uprising, the Orthodox faith was not persecuted in Hungary, since surely King Károly Róbert was preoccupied with other matters. Petrovych's revolt was just the same as those led by other oligarchs against the kings, with the goal to enlarge his power. Also, the leader of the revolt was not even Petrovych, but chancellor (*nádor*) Kopasz, who is also mistakenly identified as a Rusyn by some writers.

King Károly Róbert confiscated the land of Petrovych in 1317. Yet the fight did not end with the confiscation, because in 1320 Petrovych again invited the nobility of the county of Zemplén and Ung to fight against King Károly Róbert. However, it was not the Rusyn people who were called upon, as Mészáros and one or two Rusyn writers had thought, but rather the nobility. "Master Péter the Lieutenant-Governor of Ung and Zemplén calls upon . . . his friends, the noble lords . . . to take up arms against Róbert, who harms our possessions."[35] Thus, there was neither a national nor a religious element in Petrovych's rebellion.

(8) Prince Fedir had inherited from his father, Mykhail Koriat, the city of Navahrudak in the Grand Duchy of Lithuania following the death of his three brothers. About 1389, Fedir went to Podolia to rule.[c(c)] Vytautis (reigned 1382-1430), at the time the grand prince of Lithuania, eliminated various principalities in Lithuania and soon attacked Fedir. Despite aid from the Hungarian king, Zsigmond, in 1393 Fedir Koriatovych was forced to flee southward to Podolia. Then he came to Hungary where he was received with friendship by

---

c(c). Fedir Koriatovych (ca. 1320-1414) was the grandson of Gediminas, grand prince of Lithuania (reigned 1315-1341), a powerful state which in the course of the fourteenth century expanded its boundaries to include those principalities of former Kievan Rus' located on the territory of present-day Belorussia and the Ukraine. Koriatovych inherited both his native city of Navahrudak (in present-day Belorussia) and the land of Podolia in southwestern Ukraine. Beginning in the 1340s, he ruled both areas, and from Podolia visited on several occasions nearby Subcarpathian Rus' in Hungary. Conflict between Lithuanian princes (including the Koriatovyches) for control of the Grand Duchy of Lithuania led to the ouster of Fedir Koriatovych from Podolia in 1395. The Hungarian king Zsigmond granted Koriatovych refuge and then gave him the castle of Mukachevo, and although he spent most of his remaining years there, he retained his title as prince of Podolia where he returned on at least two occasions (1401 and 1410) to rule.

Zsigmond. Since there were hostilities between Hungary and Poland at that time, Zsigmond thought that Koriatovych would be a good tool in his hands against the Poles. Because the Lithuanian prince had fled Podolia empty-handed, Zsigmond gave him after 1395 a place to live—the estate of Mukachevo. This estate had once been owned by two queens of Hungary, Elisabeth [the wife of Károly Róbert] and Mary of Anjou (reigned 1382-1395). Several surviving documents reveal how Elisabeth and Mary attended to business as lords of Mukachevo. When Mary died in 1395, Mukachevo reverted to the crown, allowing Zsigmond to dispose of the estate as he wished. The first time the name of Fedir/Theodor as a great lord residing in Hungary occurs in documents issued by Zsigmond is in the year 1398. Later, in 1401, a scroll names Fedir for the first time as *dominus de Munkach* (lord of Mukachevo). Then, in 1400, 1404, from 1406 to 1408, and in 1411 he is cited as lieutenant-governor of the county of Bereg. Furthermore, in 1404 he was at the same time lord lieutenant of Bereg and Szatmár counties. During his stay in Hungary, Fedir Koriatovych always used the title *dux Podoliae* (prince of Podolia), by which he wanted to show that he was the legal ruler of Podolia.

According to all known authentic documents, Fedir Koriatovych lived in Hungary from the end of the fourteenth to the second decade of the fifteenth century. His title in all [Hungarian] documents is *dominus de Munkach* and not *dux de Munkach* (that is, lord, not prince of Mukachevo). Furthermore, Zsigmond writes in a document of 1419 that Fedir Koriatovych was only the governor of the Mukachevo castle, which was owned by the king: *gubernator castri nostri Munkacs*.

Despite all this, the forged foundation document for the monastery at Mukachevo was dated 1360, and in it Fedir Koriatovych is called *dei gratia dux de Munkach* (prince of Mukachevo by the grace of God). According to the contents of the foundation document, Fedir Koriatovych founded an Eastern-rite monastery, he settled Rusyn monks there, and he provided donations for the upkeep of the villages of Bobovyshchi (Borhalom) and Lavky (Lanka).

Petrov and Hodinka proved through historical arguments that every line of the [monastery foundation] document is a crude forgery. Ivan Kholodniak, a professor at Moscow University and an excellent paleographer, proved by the style and lettering of the document that it could not have derived from the fourteenth century. Some Rusyn and Slav writers, however, did not want to accept the truth. They continued to argue that the Basilian monastery of Mukachevo was founded by Koriatovych in 1360, and that he brought 40,000 men with him from Podolia to Subcarpathia, even though in fact the unfortunate Fedir was lucky to save his own skin with a fast escape!

The forged foundation document of Koriatovych was fabricated at the Mukachevo monastery. The pious monks did their best to make the document acceptable as a reliable text and to surround the name Koriatovych with a glow. The legends found in Rus' chronicles and in the lives of saints were presented to the faithful as actual events in which Koriatovych supposedly took part.

The monks actually displayed great zeal in the composition of legends. The last of these was invented by Anatolii Kralyts'kyi, archimandrite at the monastery during the mid-nineteenth century, and it was published in 1874 under the title *Litopys'* (Chronicle) of Mukachevo in the newspaper *Slovo*. The Chronicle supposedly represented the oldest linguistic relic of the Subcarpathian Rusyns. This argument was accepted by Rusyns even though no one ever saw the original. In part, [Kralyts'kyi's] chronicle read:

> Fedir Koriatovych was first voivoda of Navahrudak, later in Podolia he was voivoda and governor. Leaving his homeland of Podolia because of his uncle Algirdas, he came to Uhro-Rus' in the year 1339 to Károly I, king of Hungary, who greeted him heartily and gave him the entire Mukachevo district with all the villages in Bereg county and the towns from the Uzh river to Khust in Máramaros county. He built the town of Mukachevo in 1399, which stands even today. After living there for awhile, he went hunting on a hill that is called Chernecha Hora [Monk's Hill], and there a large dragon (*drakon*) attacked him opening its mouth wanting to swallow him. Koriatovych called upon St. Nicholas for help, and, having a lance in his hand, killed the dragon. As the stone sculpture shows in the old church, he escaped death from the mouth of the dragon, and this is also shown in the painting. In memory and respect, he built this church to Nicholas, the saint of Christ, and he brought monks there on March 8, 1360. . . . Nobody knows who the archimandrites were at the time the monastery was built, because there were devastating attacks by Tatars and Turks who ravaged the houses of the monks, by heretics who attacked church and God, put the church to the torch, stoned to death the monks, and suffocated them in fire and water. This place was so devastated that no writing remained, but oral legends preserved everything until 1458 when the chronicle begins.[36]

Kralyts'kyi's first intention in fabricating this chronicle was to make the tales regarding the foundation of the monastery appear credible, and then to prove that the Rusyns had been living since ancient times in Subcarpathian Rus'. The forgery is awkward, however, for not only is the historical data untrue, the language does not fit fifteenth-century style. As part of this discussion of the illusory and forged proofs in this document, I have intentionally used the argumentation of Petrov and other Slavic scholars, since no one can accuse Petrov, or Kholodniak, or Vasylenko of disliking the Rusyns or of having a Hungarian bias.

(9) It is common knowledge among Slavs living in foreign countries that Ungvár (now Uzhhorod) is considered the capital city of the Rusyns. For this reason many even in Hungary think Uzhhorod is a Rusyn place. However, Uzhhorod never had, nor does it now have [in 1939] a Slavic character.

We do not know when the town became into being. According to the Anonymous Chronicle, there was a castle in existence as early as the invasion of Hungary by the Magyars. This reference by Anonymous stimulated the imagination of some Rusyn and Ukrainian writers, who promoted Ungvár in their writings as the seat of Rusyn ruling princes. But since it had a Hungarian name [Ungvár], they created the Slavic form Uzhhorod. The truth of the matter is that in all documents, without exception, it is called Ungvár [meaning: castle on the Ung/Uzh river], and until the Czech occupation not only the Rusyns but also all other Slavic peoples knew it as Ungvár.

The name Uzhhorod first appeared in the mid-nineteenth century, but even so it was not adopted by the Rusyns, although their two priest writers, Anatolii Kralyts'kyi, archimandrite of the Basilian monastery in Mukachevo, and Ievhenii Fentsik, a deacon and clergyman, did their best to introduce the name into the general knowledge of the Rusyns. For instance, "Laborets', the Ruling Prince," was the title of a short story written by Kralyts'kyi. Despite being a very weak composition, it had a large impact during the Czech occupation because it claimed that Subcarpathia was a Rusyn principality before the invasion of the Magyars. The last Rusyn ruling prince, Laborets', the story goes, had his headquarters in the castle of Uzhhorod. The Magyars occupied the castle, and Laborets' tried to escape, but he was captured and sent to the gallows near the river which had been named after him. This impossible story by Kralyts'kyi was believed by many. First published in 1863 in the L'viv newspaper *Slovo* in Galicia, it was reprinted in 1925, and it has since been translated into Czech.

Ievhen Fentsik systematically called Ungvár, Uzhhorod, until the end of the nineteenth century, and he even wrote an ode entitled "Uzhhorod." Nevertheless, Slavic writers themselves admitted that the name Uzhhorod was a recent invention. In his "Ethnographic Map of Hungarian Rus'," published in 1910, Stepan Tomashivs'kyi wrote: "The name Uzhhorod which we are using instead of Ungvár, is actually not found among the [Rusyn] masses; it [Uzhhorod] is only a literary translation. However, there is no reason to reject it, especially since it was introduced by the Uhro-Rusyns themselves."[37] This invented and historically unfounded name was made official by the Czechs, and so for twenty years Subcarpathia, named *Podkarpatská Rus*, had its capital called Uzhhorod.

Apart from the [Uzhhorod] castle, nothing suggests olden times. Nothing is older than 150 years. There are many reasons for this. Ungvár was not a free city with burghers, but a fort built to control and to close, if necessary, the road leading from the Uzhok pass to the great Hungarian Plain. The present castle was built by the Drugeth counts in the fourteenth century. Beyond the inner gate can still be seen the seven thrushes and three clasps of the coat of arms of the Drugeths. From the beginning of the fourteenth century until 1679, the Drugeths were the masters of the castle and of the county. After the male line of the Drugeth family died out, Emperor Leopold (reigned 1685-1705) appointed count Miklós Bercsényi lieutenant-governor of the county of Ung and granted him the castle, its lands, and its possessions. Bercsényi was the husband of Christine Drugeth. Grand Old Miklós Bercsényi (Nagy Bercsényi Miklós), as he was called by the Magyars, held this office until 1711. Since he joined [the revolution of] Ferenc Rákóczi II and was his procurator and the leader of his armies, Bercsényi had to flee to Poland after the peace of Szatmár in 1711. The Uzhhorod castle and its belongings then reverted to the crown.

From 1711 on, Austrian troops were housed in the castle and did not take care of the palace of Bercsényi nor of its inventory. Then Empress Maria Theresa (reigned 1740-1780) donated the castle as well as the former Jesuit house and church to the Greek Catholic Eparchy of Mukachevo. Since 1778, the Greek Catholic Seminary is located in the former Bercsényi palace. It is still a fine building, despite the fact that the most interesting part, the former hall of the knights, had already been demolished and rebuilt in a different style. The most important event in the history of the castle of Uzhhorod, which lasted for several centuries, was the church union which was signed in 1646. At that time, the former Rusyn Orthodox priests decided to accept the Pope as their head and became Catholic.

That this city, founded by Hungarians and still Hungarian was designated to be the capital city of the Rusyns is entirely the result of coincidence. When in 1711, the intervention of Maria Theresa led Pope Clement XIV (reigned 1769-1774) to establish the Greek Catholic Eparchy of Mukachevo, it became necessary to establish a cathedral, apartments for canons, and other buildings for episcopal institutions. The poor Rusyns could not pay for this from their own pockets, so Empress Maria Theresa donated the castle of Uzhhorod with all buildings that belonged to it, as well as the former Jesuit house and church. Thus, the empress located in a Hungarian city the eparchy of the Rusyns because there was no other place where the necessary buildings could be found.

To secure the goods necessary for the upkeep of the diocese, Maria Theresa donated the estate of the Tapolca [Roman Catholic] abbot, near Miskolc, which meant that he assigned to Rusyns land located far from Rusyn territory—in a Hungarian region. Therefore, one should not conclude that since the monastery of Tapolca belongs to the Eparchy of Mukachevo that its territory is Rusyn land, any more than one may conclude that the headquarters of the eparchy is proof that Uzhhorod is Rusyn. Even so, the Rusyns and other Slavs have used this argument to prove that Uzhhorod is a Rusyn settlement.

CHAPTER FOUR

The Origin of the Rusyns
and Their Name

The Rusyns are the westernmost fragment of the East Slavs. The people call themselves Rusyn, Rusniak, sometimes Rusnak. Writers have given them the name *Uhrorus'* (Hungarian-Rus'). The origin of the words Russian, Rusyn, Ruthenian is northern Germanic, or Scandinavian.

There is an interesting history which explains how the largest Slavic linguistic family got its name from a small Germanic tribe. In the eighth century, when today's Russians, Ukrainians, Rusyns, and Belorussians—that is, the East Slavs—began their historical existence, they had neither a common name nor any organized formal state. There was perpetual strife between tribes and villages. The Kiev Chronicle of the twelfth century, the so-called Nestor Chronicle,[dd] tells of Slavic tribes living around Lake Ilmen, who, having had enough of the perpetual discord, unified and went "overseas" [across the Baltic] to the *Ruotsi* (Rus') Scandinavian tribe and told them: "Our land is great and rich, but there is no order in it. Come to rule and reign over us."[38]

This Scandinavian tribe, the Rus', accepted the invitation and occupied first the area around Lake Ilmen [just south of Novgorod] and the Dnieper river, so that the whole region was organized with Kiev as its center. The Rus' (in Finnish: *Ruotsi*), that Scandinavian seafaring folk which settled the shores of the Dnieper under the leadership of Riuryk (d. 879),[ee] had originally lived on the eastern shores of Sweden, which today is Uppland, Södermanland, and the island of Gotland.

---

dd. The earliest versions of what is known today as the *Primary Chronicle (Povest vremmenykh let)* were begun in the second half of the eleventh century, and one of its most important editions was copied by the Kievan monk Nestor, whose name is often given to the chronicle.

ee. Riuryk (in Scandinavian: Hroerker) was according to the *Primary*

The territory occupied and governed by them, the East Slavic land, received the name 'the land of the *Ruotsi*, land of the Rus','' in Slavic *Ruskaia zemlia*, or for short Rus'. The Scandinavians who founded the Rus' homeland were small in number, and after one or two decades they merged with the Slavic majority among whom they lived without leaving a trace. The grandchildren of the occupying Rus' chieftains became pure Slavs.

After the Rus' of Germanic origin completely merged with East Slavs, the administratively organized territory, that is the principality of Kiev, received the name Rus' (Kievskaia Rus') and its inhabitants, notwithstanding their origin, were called *rusyn/rus'kii*, or in Latin: *Russus/Ruthenus/Rutenus*. A treaty signed in 912 with the [Byzantine] Greeks by Oleg (reigned ca. 882-912) ruling prince of Kiev, identified at that time the population of the principality of Kiev as Rusyns.

Until the twelfth century, only the principality of Kiev bore the Rus' name; however, this identification gradually was taken over by other East Slav principalities during the twelfth century. Many examples can be found of the phenomenon whereby peoples and nations carry the name of other peoples. The French got their name from the Germanic Franks; the Prussians from the Lithuanian Prus; the Bulgars, from an extinct Turkic tribe called Bulgars; while the region of Lombardy recalls the Longobards.

In the thirteenth century, the Mongolo-Tatars devastated Kiev. From the ruins of Kievan Rus', two new Slavic states arose: the principality [and later kingdom] of Galicia-Volhynia in the southwest; and the Vladimir, later Muscovite principality in the north. The Galician-Volhynian principality regarded itself as the legal successor of all Kievan Rus', but since it was smaller, it was called *Mala Rus'* (Little Rus').[ff] Meanwhile, the Muscovite principality became stronger and larger. In order to distinguish it from Galicia-Volhynia (i.e., Little

---

Chronicle one of three brothers invited to rule over the Slavic and Finnic tribes in what is today northwestern Russia. He was later depicted by chroniclers and historians as the founder of the first East Slavic/Russian ruling dynasty, the Riurykoviches.

ff. Actually, the terms *Mala Rus'* and *Velika Rus'* have nothing to do with the size of either Galicia-Volhynia or Muscovy. Rather, they evolved from Byzantine Greek ecclesiastical sources and reflected a relationship to the center of the Orthodox world—Constantinople. Thus, the Orthodox region closest to Constantinople, Galicia-Volhynia in the south, was called *Mikrā Rosiia*—inner or Little Rus'; the more distant Muscovy in the north became *Megalē Rosiia*—outer or Great Rus'.

Rus'), the [Byzantine] Greeks named Muscovy *Velika Rus'* (Great Rus'). Consequently, the inhabitants of Little Rus' were called Little Russians and those of Great Rus', Great Russians. It is these names that were adopted by East Slavic literature and by the official world.

The Hungarian public and Hungarian documents until the end of the eighteenth century identified only the inhabitants of Kiev and of the Galician-Volhynian principality as the Rus', while the people of the Muscovite principality were called *Muszka* or *Moszkovita* (Muscovites). The people of the Kiev principality and later the Galicia-Volhynian principality continued to call themselves *rusyn*, while the Moscovites called themselves *russkii*. In 1667, the larger part of Little Rus' joined Great Rus'. Thereafter, in order to distinguish themselves from the Rus'/*russkii* of Muscovy, the Rusyns who lived in the south adopted the name Ukrainian; only the Galician and Hungarian Little-Rus' call themselves Rusyns (in Latin: *Ruthenus*; and in Hungarian: *Rutének*).

The traditional terms Hungarian Russian (*magyarorosz*), Little Russian *(kirsorosz)*, Rusyn *(ruszin)*, Ruthene *(rutén)* all refer to the same people. Those Little Russians (Rusyns, Ruthenes) who called themselves Ukrainians, dreamed about an independent Ukrainian state. Consequently, the word Ukrainian has taken on a chauvinistic connotation.

To distinguish themselves from other Rusyns, Rusyn writers from Subcarpathia often used the name Uhrorus', which means Hungarian-Rus'. This name implies that while the people are East Slavs, they are tied to Hungary by blood, culture, economics, and history.

Until the imposed Treaty of Trianon, the Rusyn intelligentsia both in manuscripts and published works, called their people Ruthenes (*rutének*), while the plain folk always called themselves Rusyns, Rusnaks, Rusniaks. For instance, the first printed book for Subcarpathian Rusyns, the 1698 catechism of Bishop Iosyf de Camilis carries the title: *Katekhysys dlia naouky Ouhrorouskym liudem* (Catechism for the Instruction of the Hungarian Rus' People). The second printed book was prepared for the clergy in 1727: *Kratkoe prypadkov moral'nykh ili nravnich sobranie dukhovnŷm osobam potrebnoe* (A Brief Collection: Moral Precepts for the Use of the Clergy). Similarly, older Hungarian literature refers to the people as Hungarian Russians or as Russians residing in Hungary. Slavic scholarship abroad also used this name until the Czech occupation. Thus, when speaking in Hungarian, to call the people Ruthene (*rutén*) is correct, for this name corresponds to the term Rusyn in the language of the people.

CHAPTER FIVE

Rusyn Ethnographic Groups

At various times and from different places in Galicia-Volhynia, which later became part of Poland, the ancestors of the Rusyns emigrated to Subcarpathia. For reasons already explained, they kept their tribal characteristics and dialects in their new homeland and did not fuse into a nation.

We can distinguish between two main groups according to geographical placement. Close to the Hungarian plains on the flatlands and low foothills were the lowland valley plain dwellers, while near the ridges of the Carpathians, in the mountainous regions, lived the people of the hills. They distinguished themselves [according to these basic geographic distinctions] in their own language as either *Dolyshniany* (Lowlanders) or *Verkhovyntsi* (Highlanders).

The Lowlanders/Dolyshniany

The greater number of Rusyns came from Galicia to occupy dominial lands, that is, lands owned by lords. If by examining clothing and observing dialects we can determine exactly from which part of Galicia the Highlanders came, we do not find corresponding tribes in Galicia for the Rusyns who dwell in the lowland southern regions of Máramaros, Bereg, Ung, and all of Ugocsa counties, that is the region along the former no-man's land line. Thus, we have to look for their ancestral home elsewhere. The clue is in the language.

We must look for the ancestral home of the *Lowlanders/Dolyshniany* in [northern] Volhynia's Polissia region and in Podolia. The *Dolyshniany* sound the etymological long *o* in a closed syllable as *ó, ö, u* or *ü*, and instead of *e*, they say *iu* or *iü*. In all other Rusyn and Ukrainian dialects, the sound is an *i*. For example, the Russian *kon'* (horse), sounds in Rusyn and Ukrainian dialects *kin'* (pronounced: keen), yet in one or two districts of Polissia and among the [Subcarpathian] *Dolyshniany* the phonetic form is *kon', kön', and kün'*.[39]

Furthermore, we find other traces which lead us to determine the migration pattern of the *Dolyshniany*. Most likely, these Rusyns came via Moldavia and Transylvania to Subcarpathia, and it is very probable that they spent a long time in what today is called the land of the Szeklers[gg] in Transylvania before migrating from there northward to their present territory. For example, Háromszék county [in Transylvania] has many place names of Slavic origin, and several Rusyn words unknown in other Hungarian dialects appear in the Szekler dialect. There are also several words which do not systematically occur in Subcarpathian Rusyn dialects, but they do occur in the *Dolyshniany* speech and perhaps in the dialects of the Hutsuls who also came from Moldavia—first to the headwaters of the Prut and Cheremosh Rivers, and from there to the headwaters of the Tysa.

The Szeklers call woollen pants *harisnya*; the Rusyn equivalent is *kholoshni*. Yet this word is known only in the southern parts of Podolia, among the Szeklers, and among the *Dolyshniany*. The Szekler calls breakfast *ebéd* like the *Dolyshniany* Rusyns, while the other Rusyns and the Magyars call the midday meal *délebéd* (midday lunch). It is significant that we find in the language of the *Dolyshniany* and the Hutsuls many words which occur in fourteenth-fifteenth-century documents of Moldavia and which are entirely unknown by other Rusyns; for instance, *kvar, hitlen, tokmezh, tukma, vamesh, zhold, vig* (linen on the yard) *terh* (burden), and others. Until the eighteenth century, the *Dolyshniany* maintained ties with the [Orthodox] Church of Moldavia, which proves their origin. On the other hand, the highlander Rusyns received in the old days their priests from Galicia. It is interesting to note that the Stauropegial Institute [in L'viv], which played such an important role in the life of the Galician Rusyns and paid much attention to the Rusyn highlanders, had no connection with the *Dolyshniany*, who did not even know of its existence. The Koriatovych legend is an indirect proof of this. According to that legend, 40,000 people came with Koriatovych, prince of Podolia, and in the fourteenth century they settled in the southeast corner of Subcarpathia, which is the territory of the *Dolyshniany*. While there is no doubt that not a single man came along with the Podolian prince, who was escaping from his country, the importance of the legend is the statement that Podolia is

---

gg. The Szeklers (in Hungarian: *Székely*) are a distant Hungarian group that settled in the mountainous region of eastern Transylvania (today Romania).

the ancestral homeland of the *Dolyshniany*. Podolia and Volhynia as
the ancestral homeland was a living fact in the memory of the oldest
immigrants, but later, when the great-grandchildren no longer knew
the details of the immigration, they related the arrival of their
ancestors [in Subcarpathia] with the name of Koriatovych.

The *Dolyshniany* settled about 600-700 years ago in Subcarpathian
Rus'. Because of their continual contact with Magyars, they became in
many respects Magyar. Their way of life, housing, and dress was
basically the same as that of the Magyars. Only in religion and
language did the *Dolyshniany* Rusyns differ from the Roman Catholic
and Protestant Magyars in Tiachiv (Técső), Khust, Sevliush,
Berehovo, Mukachevo, and Uzhhorod. The *Dolyshniany* shed most
of their age-old Slavic traits and adapted Magyar features. They even
came close to the Magyar way of thinking.

The majority of Rusyns were *Dolyshniany*, and since they had
adapted so closely to the Magyars, they were from an ethnographic
point of view not as interesting as the *Verkhovyntsi* (Highlanders).
The differences [between the two] in outward appearance were great
enough to be noticed even by someone who did not speak Rusyn or
who had no idea of ethnography. Their dress, furnishings, way of life,
and customs differed. The *Verkhovyntsi* lived on oats and potatoes;
the *Dolyshniany* on corn and wheat. The diet of the lowlander
Magyars also differed from the *Dolyshniany* Rusyns in that the
Magyars made bread from wheat while the Rusyns from corn (though
recently more and more Rusyns have turned to wheat bread also).

The greatest dividing factor between Rusyns and Magyars was
religion or rather the church. The Rusyns followed the Eastern rite.
They had many holy days; they fasted a great deal; and they observed
Christmas, Easter, and other feasts at different dates than did the
Roman Catholic Magyars. While the Magyars belonged to western
culture; the Rusyns followed the eastern. With respect to cultural
geography, the Rusyns stood on the borderline of the two cultures. The
Rusyns did not turn completely away from the east, nor did they
become completely western. Thus, the lowland section of the Carpathians became the home of hesitant souls, because they never could
determine whether they belonged to the west or to the east.

The borderline between the lowlanders (*Dolyshniany*) and the
highlanders (*Verkhovyntsi*) began in the county of Máramaros at Luh
(Lonka) and ran through the villages of Bereznyky (Bereznek),
Synevyr (Szinevér), and Mizhhir''ia (Ökörmező), then on through the
county of Bereg in almost a straight line to Perechyn (Perecseny) in

the county of Ung. From there it continued to Humenné (Homonna) in the county of Zemplén. From this imaginary line southward lived the *Dolyshniany* (the lowlanders) and northward the *Verkhovyntsi* (the highlanders).

The lowlander Rusyns were almost uniform in habits, morals, and dress, although there may be some insignificant language variants depending on the pronunciation of the etymological *o* in a closed syllable, which may sound either as an *o/ö* or *u/ü*.

The Highlanders/Verkhovyntsi

The *Verkhovyntsi* can be divided into several radically different and easily divisible sub-groups: (1) the Hutsuls; (2) the Boikos; and (3) the Lemkos or Lemaky.

(1) **Hutsuls**—In the forested northeastern corner of the Carpathians, at the headwaters of the Tysa in the villages of Bilyn (Bilin), Kobylets'ka Poliana (Gyertyánliget), Kosivs'ka Poliana (Kaszómező/Kaszópolyána), Iasynia, Luh (Lonka), Bohdan (Tiszabogdány), Kvasy (Tiszaborkút), Dilove (Terebesfejérpatak) and in Poienile de sub Munte (Rus'-Poliany/Havasmező), Ruscova (Ruskovo/Visóoroszi) and Repedea (Rus'-Kryvyi/Oroszkő) which are now part of Romania, there lived the smallest and most interesting branch of the Rusyns, the Hutsuls. Today there are about 30,000 of them.

The Hutsuls had emigrated from Galicia and Bukovina slowly and without being noticed between the sixteenth and nineteenth centuries. At the outset of the sixteenth century, the headwaters of the Tysa river were still uninhabited, roadless territories where Rusyn and Romanian shepherds grazed their flocks on the thick and moist grass. The borderline of Hungary was the ridge of the Carpathians, but because the Hungarian borderguards were stationed farther south in the in-habited land near Bychkiv (Bocskó), the shepherds from neighboring Galicia, Bukovina, and Moldavia could freely approach the pastures with their sheep. The upper Tysa territory stood under the administra-tion of the Coştiui (Ronaszék) Salt Office as the property of the treasury (*bona cameralia* or *bona sacrae cotonae*). It can be seen in the writings of the Salt Office that the first Rusyns settled at Rakhiv, where in 1598 fourteen shepherds lived, while at the same time the treasury found only one at Dilove. The fourteen shepherds paid taxes, which meant they must have dwelled there for at least twelve years before 1598. The one Rusyn at Dilove had a twelve-year tax exemp-tion, which means he would become a permanent resident in that year.

The owners of the shepherds and flocks slowly and gradually populated the land where Hutsuls live today. According to a Hutsul legend, the shepherds had bragged in Galicia and Bukovina about the rich pastures, the healthy air, and the springwater with healing power at the two headwaters of the Tysa. Consequently, more and more Galician and Bukovinian peasants packed up all they had and moved in.

Along with the shepherds came many draftdodgers and petty criminals who found new homes along the headwaters of the Tysa. Because the boundaries of Hungary, Poland, and Turkey met at the headwaters of the Tysa and the Prut Rivers, the Chornahora (Black Mountain) range and area around it offered many hideouts for suspicious people of all kinds, and as a result the Rusyn outlaws earned the nickname *chorni khloptsi*.

There were two kinds of outlaws or brigands (*oprishky*). A larger number were ordinary criminals; a smaller number were those who, due to unfortunate circumstances, became brigands (*oprishky*) but who supposedly were able to do good deeds. The brigands helped the poor and protected the supressed. They did not commit murder, and robbed only those noblemen and merchants on whom they wanted revenge. Originally the *oprishky* were escapees who had fled from cruel Polish landlords, or from the long military service, or from the merciless hand of the law. In the woods of the Chornahora region they formed bands which caused fear throughout a wide territory. From Sighet (Máramarossziget) in Subcarpathia to Deliatyn in Galicia they threatened public safety. However, the common people considered them heroes, and stories about the *oprishky* form part of the mainstream of Hutsul folk poetry. Even today most songs, the nicest ballads, and stories are about the *oprishky*.

The first brigand leader (*oprishok*) to become famous was Ivan Pisklyvyi in 1703, followed by Pinta in 1704. The best known *oprishok*, who is most popular in the memory of the Hutsuls and of whom even today the Hutsul mother tells tales to her child, is Oleksa Dovbush. He led his gang from 1738 until 1744, when he was killed by one of his own men. According to legend, his band consisted of thirty members all on horseback. It is said about them that "they robbed the rich and supported the poor. Sin therefore was not committed." Moreover, they often donated to religious purposes. The Hutsuls of Rakhiv believe as fact that Dovbush gave the money for their church bells. One storyteller in Rakhiv, Vintoniek the bellringer, who is an authority in the village, swore an oath to prove that he told the truth.

All in the village believe him, for after all, he was old and experienced. When he was young he had served in the army and had been in Milan, Vienna, and other great cities. The population of Rakhiv said of him: "He was smart and knew a lot." Vintoniek explained to the villagers that the origin of the name Rakhiv (actually Rahó) came from the fact that Dovbush used to count their stolen money at that place. In Rusyn, *rakhuvaty* means to count, from the German *rechnen*.

The songs and tales of Dovbush recount what happened at his deathbed. When he was about to die, his comrades surrounded him to ask: "Our lord, our leader, who will lead us orphans, who will look after us?" The answer of Dovbush, lord of the brigands was: "Distribute the money among yourselves, get married, settle along the fast-running waters of the Tysa, and live like decent shepherds and farmers."

The romantic world of brigandry lasted in the country of Máramaros until the end of the eighteenth century, when most brigands married and settled into a law abiding life. Nobody would believe that some present-day Hutsuls had outlaw ancestors.

Because in the Romanian language highway robbers were called *hoc-ul* or *huc-cul*, the Rusyns dwelling at the headwaters of the Tysa were labelled by this name. Originally it was a nickname, but later it became a name for an ethnic group. Slavic literature took the name from the Romanians and gradually it was given to the Hutsuls. However, they never used this expression when talking about themselves and hated to be called such. The name is not an old one, for Haquet, a former professor at the University of L'viv who wrote about them at the end of the eighteenth century, did not know the term.

From a linguistic and an ethnographic standpoint, the Hutsuls differed markedly from the other Slavs, forming therefore a distinct Rusyn tribe. One or two amateur writers doubted their Slavic origin and thought they originated from the Uzh, the Pechenegs, and God knows what other people. These unfounded, fantastic theories were echoed even in the Hungarian press.

Ethnographic research, mainly the work of Volkov, has proven without doubt that the Hutsuls are not only Slavs today, but that they are of Slavic origin as well. Their differences from other Rusyns can be explained by their geographical position as well as by their contact with Romanians and Magyars among which races they were also slightly intermixed.

Originally the Hutsul was a shepherd and farmer. Today, he is an excellent lumberjack and raftsman (a craft learned from the Germans). [The German presence came] after the defeat of Rákóczi in 1711, when Subcarpathia lacked manpower, mainly master craftsmen. As an incentive, Law 108 of 1723 allowed six years of tax exemption to immigrants who came on their own account, while the Austrian state treasury gave German skilled workmen and master craftsmen even more concessions: free building lots, land, lumber and fuel. A church was even erected for them and their clergy were paid. Soon after the law had been approved, German settlers came to Iasynia and built the first large dam and sluice on the Chorna Tysa upstream from Lazeshchyna. Later the treasury built more dams along the course of the Chorna and Bila Tysa rivers and its tributaries in order to permit the use of rafts at low water periods. Two or three times a week the gates of the dams were opened so that the water that poured out would swell the river for about twelve hours, thus permitting the rafts to slide quickly through to the next gate. This was almost a revolutionary innovation, and it permitted the transportation of lumber from the virgin forests of Subcarpathia to the great Hungarian plain.

The planned exploitation of forests began in the time of Maria Theresa and Joseph II, that is, between 1740 and 1790. These rulers of Hungary settled Austro-German lumbermen from Gmünd, Bad Ischl, and Ebensee in the Hutsul villages of Bohdan and Rakhiv. Because the German craftsmen were few and expensive, the treasury decided to train Hutsuls to become lumberjacks and raftsmen. It is from this time that the Hutsuls became serfs of the treasury. All who were on the enumeration list received 35 acres of land for clearing and use for their own purposes; further, they were given permission to build permanent homes, free pasturing rights in the alpine slopes, and the use of as much lumber and fuelwood as needed in the household. In turn, the Hutsuls had to work 100 days a year at a job and in a place assigned by the treasury. The job might be lumbering, road building, river-flow correction, or rafting, crafts taught them by the German settlers. Before that time the Hutsuls did not know of the existence of the saw and did all their woodwork with the ax. The Hutsuls were good pupils, because in time they became master lumberjacks and famous raftsmen.

The immigration from Galicia and Bukovina continued; therefore, from time to time the treasury ordered a new census and then engaged the newcomers to work. For example, in Iasynia, between 1774 and 1828, 145 new treasury workers were enlisted from recently immigrated Hutsuls, and in 1836 another 76.

Originally the Hutsuls were a horseback-riding folk. They rode up the alpine slopes to neighboring villages, and in earlier times even went on horseback to church for weddings. Today they mostly walk, because they have become impoverished and have no money for horses. Often they complain to good friends that they hardly ever have a horse and cannot carry a gun. After "Kossuth's war" [1848-1849], orders from the gendarmerie took their guns away and never returned them. Yet the Hutsul feels he is a "real man" only if he has a gun. The Hutsul ax, the *toporets'*, is not enough, for an ax cannot make the kind of bang that causes mountains to echo.

The Hutsuls are among the more attractive people—well-built, wide-shouldered, muscular, tall, and slim. The average height of men is 169.5 cm. and women 155.6 cm. as opposed to the average height of Polish and Russian men which is only 165.5 cm. A fiery eye sparkles under the Hutsul's dense eyebrows. His hair and eyes are dark. As high as 83.3 percent of the men and 66.7 percent of the women have brown hair, while 2.8 percent are blonde. Old men wear their hair hanging down to the shoulders, while the new generation cuts its hair. It is interesting to note that Hutsuls do not get bald. Hutsul women indeed deserve the description—"the beautiful sex." Their faces are white, their figures slim, and they smile a great deal as though quite conscious of their beauty.

With few exceptions, the Hutsuls were Greek Catholic. They held strongly to their faith, especially to ceremonies. Yet, at the same time, the Hutsul was also superstitious. He would not have thought of weddings, baptisms, or funerals without a priest and the church. Moreover, Christmas is an adult celebration, not one for children. There were no Christmas trees and there were no presents for the children. According to an ancient Hutsul custom, a lavish dinner was to be eaten at Christmas. The rule—at least for those who could afford it—was to prepare twelve different courses. However, this multi-course dinner could hardly be called a Lucullian feast, since there was no variety and it was not particularly tasty.

Normally, the main staple of the Hutsuls is *kulesha*, a sort of porridge cooked from cornmeal. It was stirred until firm and eaten with milk or cottage cheese. Other foods served as daily nourishment for Hutsuls were cheese, milk, potatoes, eggs (mostly scrambled), beans, cabbage, stuffed cabbage, noodles, and oat or corn griddle-cakes rather than bread. Meat was eaten only at great festivals. The Hutsul was hospitable and liked to invite strangers to his table. He also loved to tell tales, to sing, and to make songs which, however, were not very musical.

Hutsuls built their houses out of spruce and used boards for roofing. Though the inside was often white-washed, the exterior was unfinished. The home consisted of three parts: the living quarters, a covered porch (*pitvar*), and pantry. In the living quarters was a longish brick-oven which also served as bed along with another rough hewn bed, a table, one or two chairs, benches along the walls, and a small cabinet for the dishes. The house usually had no chimney, so that the smoke escaped through the roofing of the porch.

The Hutsul loved freedom. He strove to make his children independent from parental supervision as soon as possible, yet the child who would inherit the house stayed at home. The Hutsul was very talented. He was a handy carpenter, cartwright, and wheelmaker. Although there were one or two blacksmiths among the Hutsuls, other crafts were not found. Hutsuls were master carvers, and the village of Bilyn and the sub-alpine region in general are still adorned by pagoda-like, wooden churches that are marvels of folk-art. The women made wonderful needlework, embroidery, and sewing, as is evident from the shirt-sleeves, shoulders, and the front of their clothes. Almost all pieces of wearing apparel were embroidered.

Men wore trousers made of red or black raw wool. In the summer, they went sleeveless; in the winter, with sleeves and a long vest made of sheepskin—the *kozhukh* or a black tunic (*serdak*) of raw wool. The same clothing was worn winter and summer, in rain or snow. In warm weather, they turned the tunic inside out to expose the sheep fur lining.

Hutsuls loved glossy, colorful ornaments. The small leather pouch worn at the side and the knife-holder had copper inlay, metal buttons, or coins sewn on. The wide leather belt with a holster on it—in which usually a hunting knife was inserted—was the pride of the Hutsul man. His highest hope was to possess a gun.

The women wore a garment that went to the ankles and was richly ornamented with embroidery. Over the shirt was worn a thick, homespun, ankle-length apron which was richly ornamented both front and back. Leather mocassin-like shoes (*bochkory*) were worn. Those who were better off wore laced or riding boots. They had a nice ribbon around their neck, richly ornamented with beads.

Hutsul women never rested; they worked even when on the street. A staff with a handle was fastened to their belts on the left side, so they could spin thread and wind the thread on the spindle. It is interesting to note that whether the Hutsul woman was proudly walking on the street or riding like a man, she could turn the spindle without stopping.

The main occupations of the Hutsul were animal husbandry, lumbering, and rafting. During the three- to four-month-long summer season, beef cattle went to the pastures where they remained in the custody of cowherds. The owner of the beef cattle or one of his family members went up the alpine slopes only to collect and bring home their share of cheese and goat's cheese (brynza).

The alpine shepherd's life was quite difficult. In the daytime, he remained outside, even in the wind and rain; at night, he slept in a hut where wind and rain would penetrate. To repel pestering insects, he would soak his shirt in boiling butter and would wear it until it fell off in rags. Primarily a shepherd, the Hutsul did not understand dairy farming, and so he gained very little income from it. At the beginning of the century, the Hungarian government organized model dairies in the Menchul range, which belong to the villages of Kvasy and Tysa-Bohdan. Excellent Emmental-type cheese and high-quality butter is still made at both places.

Horse breeding regressed, yet the small Hutsul horse (*hutsulyk*) was very strong, great in stamina, and a hard worker. Military experts in World War I stated that the *hutsulyk* had a consistent capacity for work during a 12-hour period, whether with or without food or drink. A stud-farm at Turii Remety makes great efforts today [i.e., in 1939] to supply farmers of Verkhovyna with Hustul horses. They have obtained good breeding stock and have banned the export of full-blooded Hutsul mares from Subcarpathia.

The Hutsul did not engage in trade. His only money-making occupation was lumbering and rafting. During the winter he worked in the woods cutting spruce, sliding the cut spruce down the valley, removing the bark, and tying the peeled logs into rafts. From spring to fall, rafts were floated down the Tysa. Rafting was a dangerous occupation. A careful raftsman must slide the raft along the curving stream between sharp rocks. If the raft would collide with a rock, the raftsman would pay with his life. Even so, the Hutsul was hardy and daring. He was not afraid of death. As the proverb says: "man should be scared of life, not of death." If he confronted wolves and wrestled with bears, why should he be afraid of the Tysa, the river that brings life to Hungary? Near the source of the Tysa was the cradle of the Hutsul. Hutsuls did not go to the Great Hungarian Plain to harvest as other Rusyns did, for they did not know how to do this. They were transported by the Tysa to the plains.

The most pleasant part of the forested Carpathians was the Hutsul land, watched over by the more than 2000-meter-high peaks of

Hoverla, Pop Ivan, and Petros. The Hutsul loved his homeland ardently. When he had to leave his beloved mountains a piercing homesickness befell him. Impatiently, he waited for the day he could return. As soon as he handed over his raft, he hurried back to his village, and with the naive joy of the simple man he would say that he would not exchange his hut for the richest castle in the plains.

The Hutsul called his homeland the "land of wonders." Old folks told how God and the Devil together created the Verkhovyna from quicksand that they had brought from the sea. When the Lord God began to spread evenly the seeds of mountains and plains, the devil, transformed into a wasp, bit God's hand. Startled, the Lord God dropped the mountain seeds from his hand and they all fell on Máramaros. This explained why the land of the Hutsuls was all alpine hills and mountains. Eternal nature brought the cleanest green and blue colors and placed its mountains at the headwaters of the Tysa in the northeast Carpathians.

(2) **Boikos**—West of the Hutsuls in the highlands between the Sopurka and Laborec rivers, that is in the Verkhovyna, live the Boikos. If the proud Hutsul is the aristocrat of the highland dwelling Rusyns, the modest Boiko represents the common folk. For instance, when novelists write about the Rusyns in the forested Carpathian region, it is the Hutsuls whom they choose for their characters, as in the stories of the Ukrainians Iurii Fedkovych, Ivan Franko, Mykhailo Kotsiubyns'kyi, Hryhorii Khodkevych, and Mykhailo Staryts'kyi; the Poles Józef Krozeniowski (Joseph Conrad) and I. Turczyński; and the Germans K. C. Franzos and Blumenthal. They would not be likely to write about the poor Boiko.

The Boiko homeland is neither as pompous or overwhelming as that of the Hutsul. This is because the Vihorlat and Beskyd ranges where Boikos live are more modest and lack the magnificence and ascent of the taller mountains farther east. It seems, however, quite friendly and warm, with a series of smaller hills that look like sugar cones. The tallest, the Stoi, in the beautiful Borzhava range, is only 1,679 meters high. It is interesting to note that the waters dividing the Carpathian ranges here are intersected by lovely valleys, such as the Teresva, Tereblia, and Borzhava.

Like the name Hutsul, the name Boiko is somewhat ironic. Some suggest it comes from the Rusyn adjective *boikyi*, meaning handy or lively. Others suggest it derives from *boi*, meaning yes, that's it, an expression used frequently by Boikos. There are also other fantastic explanations as with the word Hutsul. Certainly it has nothing to do

with the Celtic *bojok*. The Boikos call themselves *Verkhovyntsi*
(Highlanders), while the neighboring lowlanders and the Hutsuls call
them Boikos. By the way, the Hutsuls mockingly call other highlander
Rusyns Boikos. The greatest insult is to call a Boiko a *pechenii boiko*,
literally a "baked Boiko," but meaning basically a dumb peasant.

Generally, the Hutsuls mock the Boikos and tease them with the
following song:

> Hey Hutsul, dear Hutsul,
> Where did you hide our Boiko?
> Did you bake him?
> Alive you ate him?
> I did not eat him
> Neither baked him,
> He was eaten by a wolf
> While mushroom picking.

A lowlander Rusyn is just as ironic when he jokingly says Boiko.
For example in this verse:

> A Boiko I am, and you are too,
> Together as Boikos we make two.
> Shake hands
> And let us dance.

The Boiko dances are very fast, involving small steps for which they
are teased by the lowlander Rusyns in a song:

> I go up in the Carpathians,
> There live the Boikos,
> Into small pieces they cut every song,
> And, still, they have a good time.

The Boiko does not have the good looks of the Hutsul and is on
average almost 5 cm. shorter. He has a wide templebone, narrow lips,
a wide chest, and strong muscles. He cannot be said to be good looking, for his countenance is not as vivid as that of the Hutsul. He
speaks slowly and in monotones. He is blonde, though in time his hair
turns brown from frequent oiling. The girls have round faces and are
quite pretty. Their main amusement is to go to the spinnery, where
they spend the evening though not always in the most enlightened
fashion.

Generally, the Boiko is talkative and friendly. His regular meeting
places are the churchyard or the tavern. There he discusses his problems and the news of the world. The Boiko is a good-hearted, depend-

able, obedient, and helpful individual. When angered, which he becomes very quickly, he brawls. He is not enterprising by nature. In this, he has a more passive nature than the Hutsul. He is willing to work when work is necessary, although he does not make much effort in that regard. He is somewhat fatalistic, easily accepting his lot. Boikos are talented, and some make good peddlers. Like the Slovak tinkerers (*drotary*) the Boikos travel long distances peddling, carrying for example Hungarian fruit to Polish markets and sometimes selling wine.

The Boiko is very poor. He cannot send his children to educational institutions other than public school; therefore, he cannot utilize his talents, even though the Boikos are talented in commerce.

Among all the Rusyns, the Boiko is the best of family men. He loves his parents and his children, and pays respect to the elderly. In case of danger or trouble, he will do the impossible to save his family. The Boiko is the only Rusyn for whom we can find traces of the ancient common household system. While the Hutsul is individualistic, the Boiko has a strong community feeling.

It is not only the old *urbaria*[hh] which mention large Boiko families. Bidermann stated as well that in his lifetime during the nineteenth century he saw three to four families living under one roof, and this is confirmed by the Czech writer Josef L. Pič.[40] The Boiko homestead community (*dvorishche*) was similar to the South Slavic homestead community, the *zadruga*. The married sons remained in their parent's home and farmed together. The head of the family was the father or the grandfather. After the death of the father, the brothers did not separate; they remained together under the leadership of the oldest brother. The oldest brother was the boss; his wife, the chief housewife. All real estate and tangible goods were commonly owned; only the dowry of the wives was private property. The head of the family disposed of the commonly-owned wealth. He distributed the workload, made purchases, and sold goods toward the common account. All obeyed the family head and stuck rigidly to traditional customs.

The memory of the homestead community still survives among Boikos. Often the married son, if he has no house, continues to live and farm with the parents until he saves enough to establish his own household. On the other hand, the Hutsul son does not want to marry

---

hh. The *urbaria* (sing.: *urbarium*) were record books prepared annually by large landed estates.

until he secures a home. In contrast, the Boiko son says he has time to obtain a house after he marries, and that in the meantime he stays with his parents. Even today [1939] the Boiko feels that the old custom was right: that the estate was left intact until it could be divided among the grandchildren at which point the communal homestead would be dissolved. Yet this old custom had to be abandoned because the wives could not get along with one another.

Since ancient times the Boiko believed that unbroken soil, forest, and free-flowing water such as a creek and river, or natural lakes are commonly-owned things. Anybody can use them if he needs them. Only what a man has made with his own hands or brain is his own. Therefore, in the forest and in the meadows anyone can pick strawberries, raspberries, blackberries, blueberries, hazelnuts, mushrooms, wild apples, and wild pears for personal use. When a Boiko needs a smaller article, say a wooden stake, and he sees one in his neighbor's courtyard, he takes it without asking or he enters his neighbor's garden or woodlot and cuts one. His neighbor will not press charges against him because he would act the same way in a similar situation. It is natural not to return quickly a borrowed small object (saw, wheelbarrow, ax, hammer). The Boiko says: "The owner will call for it when he needs it." Furthermore, he does not hesitate to lend the borrowed object to somebody else, so that the owner may have to look for it through half the village until he finds the object.

The majority of the highlander Rusyns are Boikos. They live close to the ridge of the Carpathians. They did not come there because they were invited, nor did they settle in any planned way. Between the sixteenth and eighteenth centuries, the Boikos slowly and surreptitiously infiltrated from the [neighboring] Boiko territories of Galicia, that is from the mountainous districts of Turka, Stryi, Drohobych, Dolyna, Kalush, and Sambir. They settled between the mountains, in the valleys, and on slopes near creeks.

For a long time the Boikos could freely go with their flocks to the Verkhovyna from the opposite side of the Carpathians. Initially, they could also go freely to the headwaters of the Tysa, because no one guarded the borderline at the top ridge of the Carpathians. In fact, the actual borderline was not even clearly defined. Then, when the [Austrian] treasury and the owners of estates learned that foreign shepherds frequented the alpine slopes, they soon collected taxes.

By the end of the sixteenth century, the Mukachevo-Chynadiievo estate took each summer as taxes for each flock of goats or sheep (between 500 and 600 head) one florin and one cheese. Also, when residents from Galicia mowed grass in the Hungarian Verkhovyna and wintered their flocks there, the so-called "vatra-money"—one florin for each basket (skol)—was collected. According to the 1649 Urbarium of the Mukachevo estate, strangers—whether freemen or serfs—paid three pieces of change for each head of beef cattle and one cheese for each sheep flock. Later the taxes were raised.

Many of the farmers who grazed their flocks in the Verkhovyna settled wherever they liked, and after a while Boiko mountain villages developed. More of them sprung up as immigration continued. The 1649 Urbarium also mentions Boiko settlements in Velykyi Bereznyi (Nagyberezna), Kostryna, Stavne, Volosianka. A Latin chronicle written by the pastor of Huklyvyi (Zúgó) in the eighteenth century mentions that "most likely the whole population of the entire Verkhovyna began to arrive at the beginning of the last century or not long before."[41] Very many Galician Boikos immigrated after Rákóczi's freedom struggle ended, between 1711 and 1720.

Because the Verkhovyna is suitable only for animal husbandry, this is the Boiko's primary occupation. However, they did not live exclusively from animal husbandry and shepherding either in the past or present. For instance, the Boikos on the Mukachevo-Chynadiievo and Uzhhorod estates went harvesting to the Hungarian plains from the sixteenth century onward. In the seventeenth century, landlords on the plains employed whole harvesting gangs and paid them with a percentage—a fifth, sixth, or seventh of the sheaves. The harvesters took home the threshed seed. Moreover, the landlords in the Verkhovyna liked their serfs to go away [to the plains] for temporary work, because in this way they were sure that their dues would be paid. Besides harvesting with the knowledge of their landlords, many Boikos also worked in vineyards.

Boiko young men and women enjoyed working at the harvest on the Hungarian plains. Returning home, they bragged about their knowledge of Hungarian picked up while working there. In the winter at the spinnery, many Hungarian songs were and still are recited with the original Hungarian text or in a rough translation. And if one wants to pay a compliment to a person, they say, "You are like a Hungarian."

However, the most pleasant Boiko legends are those connected with shepherding and the alpine horn [trembita].

In olden times, when all Boikos had flocks grazing in the alpine slopes, the richest farmer had a beautiful daughter who could play the *trembita* with such artistry that she expressed not only her feelings but also her thoughts. It so happened that at times robbers from Galicia attacked and drove away the flocks. One day the robbers came across the rich man's flocks and tied up the shepherds. Besides taking the sheep, they wanted to take the girl also. The girl pleaded with the robbers: 'Permit me to say good-bye to the mountains and let me play once more my *trembita*'. The robbers agreed. They were so fascinated with her sounds that nobody realized that she was warning her father about the danger. The rich man understood his daughter's call, and accompanied by the men of the village, rushed to the hills. He captured the robbers, saved his daughter, and retrieved his flocks too.

The Boikos do not engage in handicrafts. Yet no village can exist without a blacksmith, and so they say: "Every village needs a Gypsy." At Verkhnii Studenyi (Felsőhidegpatak), in 1930, there were two blacksmiths, a Gypsy and a Jew, but the people called both "Gypsies." Craftsmen in other Boiko villages are Germans or Jews.

An old adage holds that there are three things Rusyns hate: the horse, the bush, and the road. This saying is only in part true. The Hutsul, of course, adores his horse, and the lowlander Rusyn cherishes it too. However, the Boiko does not appreciate the horse, because he cannot utilize him completely. On the other hand, the Boiko treasures oxen, and profits most from them. Oxen are satisfied with grass or hay, while a horse, if it works hard at all, needs corn or oats from time to time. "If we give the horse oats or corn what remains for us?" is a typical Boiko response to the comment that their horses are often weak or skinny. Similarly, the Boiko dislikes the bush and the forest because both presented great backbreaking toil to his forefathers as they tried to eke out a plot for a house and a small field for corn or vegetables.

In the Verkhovyna, almost every foothold of soil had to be carved out of the forest. The Boikos who immigrated from Galicia cleared plots near a creek or in a valley where it widens and they erected huts nearby. The Boiko lived there in isolation, without neighbors. Later, more and more little houses were built along the creek's bank or on the hillside and a new settlement or village came into being. Streets or roads were out of the question. Traffic went along the side of the creek, from which pathways led to the houses. Later, a road was built along the creek, and the small Rusyn homes that spread all over the hillside were administratively divided into small villages. Where the terrain permitted, part of the population was transferred to the banks of the creek. Yet streets were never built, for they were impossible to build even to the present day.

The little wooden houses along the bank of the creek or on the hillside consist of three parts—a living quarter, a covered porch (*pitvar*), and a utility room. The house is furnished in the same way as the Hutsul home. The oldest and the youngest member of the family sleeps on the top of the (brick) oven. However, the house has no chimney, because the Rusyn thinks the roof is stronger if smoke penetrates it.

The nourishment for Boikos is weaker than that of the Hutsul. Their staple food is flat oat cakes. They also eat potatoes, beans, and a porridge made of cornmeal. Holiday food is scrambled egg fried in lard, matzos in milk, stuffed cabbage, noodles (*halushky*) with lard, and herring. They consider stuffed chicken a gourmet dish and serve it only at solemn occasions. For such occasions, the inner parts of the chicken are cleaned out and a stuffing of cornmeal softened with milk is packed in tightly. The opening is sewn and the chicken is first cooked, then roasted. Stuffed chicken is a dish that fulfills a Boiko's fondest dream.

While Hutsuls love their homeland and change residence only within Hutsul-inhabited areas (whether as a result of marriage or similar familial reasons), Boikos move with ease if they think their life will be better in a new environment. Many Boikos emigrated to the southern Hungarian counties of Torontál and Bács [today's Vojvodina in Yugoslavia]. They sold their belongings because they sought to buy better land elsewhere. Nonetheless, the Boiko homeland is picturesque too. From the highest peak of the Borzhava range is a beautiful panorama. The Great [Hungarian] Plain is visible toward the south, as is the surrounding Boiko-inhabited Verkhovyna and Poland in the north. The so-called Jubilee road weaves its way through the entire length of the Verkhovyna. It begins at Uzhhorod and passes the Polonyna Rivna (Rónahavas) peak, Volovets' (Volócz), the Borzhava range, and on to the land of the Hutsuls through Brustura. All along the way are alpine meadows, mountain peaks, passes, forests, and marvellous wooden churches. The Boiko region also has several rather simple spas and mineral water wells at Lumshory (Rónafüred), Poliana (Polenafürdő), Syniak (Kékesfürdő), Zan'ka (Zanyka, now in Volovets'), and Ust'-Chorna (Királymező). Yet, since it is so difficult to make a good living there, the Boiko easily can leave all that behind in the hope of a better life elsewhere.

Boikos believe autumn to be a sad time, because they then have to protect their meager crop from wild animals. From the poor soil the Boiko gathers oats, barley, potatoes, and in the valleys corn. When harvest time approaches, he has to protect his modest crop from the wild boar. Having no gun, he cannot shoot it. He tries to protect his crops by erecting a little hut in the middle of the potato field, and each evening making a big fire in front of the hut. When he hears the boar approaching, he makes noises which cause the boar to flee.

It is a sad sight to see the flaming fires on the hillsides during fall, and to hear the disturbing sounds that penetrate from the distance. The poor Boikos sit at the fireside near their huts and talk about the olden times when hunting was permitted and they could turn a profit from a boar that was shot rather than a loss. They could make boots from the hide of the boar and eat boar meat, so that in those days there was enough meat for every holiday.

(3) **Lemkos**—Farther west from the Boikos, in the hilly area between the Poprad and Latorytsia rivers on the low slopes of the Beskyd mountains, live the Lemkos. They are called Lemkos by the other Rusyns because instead of the Rusyn *lysh* (for the word: only) they say *lem* or *len*. Originally, Lemko was a nickname, like Hutsul or Boiko. Actually, the Lemkos call themselves Rusyns or Rusnaks. If one asks them whether they are Lemkos, they answer: "We are Rusyns, Rusnaks. The Lemkos live somewhere among the Boikos."

The land of the Lemkos is a low mountain range. The elevations stretch wide and long towards the west, east, and northwest. The rise in elevation is so gradual that it can be traversed easily by horse-drawn carriage, and this made contact with Lemkos [north of the mountains in Galicia] very easy. The ridge of the Carpathians is very low in this area. The Dukla Pass, for instance, is only 502 meters, and the Zboriv Pass, 592 meters above sea level.

Geography played an important role in the life of the Lemkos. From the time of their immigration to Hungary, the difficult terrain of the Carpathians had kept to a minimum contact between the Hutsuls and Boikos in Hungary and their brethren north of the Carpathians. On the other hand, the Lemkos who lived on the two sides of the low-lying Carpathians did not separate. Hence, the Galician Lemkos dwelling in the Lesko, Sanok, Krosno, Gorlice, Grzybów, Jaslo, and Nowy Sącz districts frequently visited their brothers in Hungary who often returned the visit.

In olden times, both the Lemkos of Hungary and the Lemkos of Galicia went harvesting on the Hungarian plains. Furthermore, at the beginning of the nineteenth century, many larger Hungarian estates employed Lemko swineherds from Galicia. This may explain why in the Lemko village of Mszana/Mshana in Galicia [Krosno district], many family names are Kondash. There, if one is asked where he got his name, the reply is: "One of my forefathers was a swineherd in Hungary; there they call the swineherds *kondás* [pronounced kondash]." Many Lemkos also came from Galicia to Hungary to buy things, and in older days, when formalities were less cumbersome, many married in Hungary as well.

The names of Hungarian villages occur in many [Galician Lemko] folksongs. For example, in Olchowiec/Ol'khovets' [Krosno district], they sing:

> Shedding her tears, sobbing was Hanchusha
> From Tokaj she didn't get an apple from Andrusha.
> Don't cry Hanchusha, don't be sad,
> I bring you an apple from Nowy Sącz.

Among the names of Hungarian towns, Debrecen occurs most often in the tales and songs of the Galician Lemkos, because most Lemkos went harvesting in Hajdú county, [the capital of which is Debrecen]. The Hungarian Lemkos also went northward to the Galician Lemkos to buy things and to amuse themselves. [The close ties are also evident in the fate of] an old wooden church that now stands in the village of Venecia (Venécza) in Sáros county. The church was originally built in 1654, in Nowa Wieś/Nova Ves', a Lemko village in Galicia [Nowy Sącz district]. In 1724, the people of Venecia purchased the church, took it apart, and rebuilt it in their village. They still worship in that building.

Of all the highlander Rusyns, the Lemkos came to Hungary the longest time ago. This was because the granting of estates and settling of the old no-man's land began in the thirteenth century in the far western county of Szepes (Spish), and from there it continued gradually toward the east, so that Máramaros county was settled last.

However, the Rusyns were not the first settlers in Szepes county. We know that of the 66 villages in Szepes county that date from the twelfth and thirteenth centuries, there is not a single Rusyn among them. If Rusyns had been settled there before the Tatar invasion (1241), at least one document would have mentioned them. The Rusyns came later than the Poles, Slovaks, Germans, and Magyars. As a result, they live on poor soil where hardly anything grows, since the first settlers always take the best lands, the richest plains, river valleys, or protected territories.

The counties of Szepes, Sáros, Abaúj-Torna, and Zemplén are very colorful from an ethnographic point of view. In this area of mixed languages, religious diversity, and various nationalities live Magyars,

Slovaks, Germans, Poles, and Lemko Rusyns. Many villages have a mixed population, yet there are a fair number of homogenous or predominantly Lemko villages. Szepes county has the smallest number, where twenty Lemko villages make up only seven percent of the total population. Everywhere that related peoples meet, there are areas where no one can decide to which nationality or language group the local population belongs. Therefore, in the Soviet Union, the borderline between Ukrainian and Russian [ethnolinguistic] territory is undecided, just as it is in the Balkan peninsula along the Bulgarian and Serbian linguistic border. Such race and nationality controversies cannot be decided with the tools of scholarship, since each side insists that the dialects, which in any case are usually mixed, belong to itself and does not accept any scholarly arguments to the contrary.

Rusyns think that all Greek Catholic Eastern Slovaks are of Rusyn origin. They have been Slovakized, so the Rusyns claim. This statement is erroneous. Religion cannot be accepted as a distinguishing mark between nationalities or races. If there are in Subcarpathia not only Rusyns but also Romanians and Magyars who are Greek Catholic or Orthodox, then national origin does not explain why there are Slovaks of the Eastern rite. It is known that during the Counter-Reformation in Szepes and Sáros (Sharysh) counties, several Protestant villages and Slovak villages became Greek Catholic.

The principle *cuius regio—eius religio* [he who rules the territory determines the religion] was in effect in some cases among the Lemko Rusyns. Upon the order of Mykhail Ol'shavs'kyi, bishop of Mukachevo between 1750 and 1767, all parishes in Zemplén, Sáros, Szepes, and Abaúj counties were investigated. On the basis of the bishop's visits (*visitatio canonica*), a survey was compiled which contained the names of parishes and affiliated churches, the foundation dates of church buildings, the condition of the structures, and an inventory of the equipment. The survey also reported when and by whom churches were consecrated and what the parishioners' obligations were toward their priests and parishes. One or two surveys contain as well other interesting information.

A survey recorded at Cernina (Czernina) near Humenné stated: "From time immemorial it is said the stone church was built by Roman Catholics. The Lutherans then seized it. Later, some fifty years ago, the completely-ruined building was repaired by Rusyn parishioners, and since then it is used undisturbed by them." With regard to the village of Lenartov (Lenartó), the survey states: "the stone church was founded by parishioners of the Roman rite, but for many years a Greek Catholic priest read mass there." According to the record book of Malcov (Malczó), "the stone church was built by Roman Catholics, then it became a Lutheran place of worship, and about thirty years ago the landlord gave it to the Greek Catholic Rusyns." Similarly, in the survey book from Petjanki (Peklén, today Uzovské Pekl'any) we read: "the wooden church . . . was eight years ago seized from the Lutherans by the landlord."[42]

Without doubt many Rusyns and Poles assimilated with the Eastern Slovaks. This was a voluntary process, which Rusyns and Poles welcomed. It is interesting to review the findings of Czambel regarding the reasons for the increase in Slovakization.[43]

The first reason is that Rusyns considered the Slovak language to be aristocratic as compared to the Rusyn or Polish languages. The second reason is that before World War I, many pamphlets, books, flyers, and anthologies of folklore were printed in the Slovak language, while Rusyn language editions were a rarity. Moreover, Slovak priests, Slovak landlords, and their family members spoke with Poles and Rusyns only in Slovak. If before the war a Magyar family wanted to teach a Slavic language to its children, they hired a Slovak nursemaid, never a Rusyn or a Polish one. People saw this and therefore regarded the Slovak language, in contrast to Rusyn and Polish, as a more prestigious way of speaking. Consequently, Rusyn boys and girls tried to talk with each other the way the "better class" did. They preferred to do this even more if there was a Rusyn priest in the family, because they spoke Hungarian with rare exception.

It is evident that those Rusyns who lived among Slovaks or in the vicinity of [East] Slovak territory did not maintain their own [Rusyn] language. That language was not respected by their own priests who for the most part could not even speak it correctly. That the Rusyns who lived in eastern Slovakia became in time Slovaks was, therefore, a natural development, especially since Slovak culture was more highly advanced than Rusyn.

The Polish language, like Slovak, had a very strong influence on the language of the Lemkos. Only one or two words of Polish origin are found in Hutsul and Boiko dialects, having been brought by them when they immigrated and never forgotten. In contrast, the language of the Lemkos is full of Polish words. So great was the influence of the Polish way of thinking and speaking that it affected the accent. In all [East Slavic] dialects, whether Russian, Ukrainian, or Rusyn, the accent varies. The only exception is found in the Lemko dialects, where the accent falls consistently on the penultimate syllable just as in Polish.

Like the other Rusyns, the Lemkos are mainly an agricultural people. They till the soil and raise animals. However, because their soil is
heavy with clay, poor in minerals, and full of stones, they raise just
enough to survive. They sow the same crops as Slovaks living nearby—oats, corn, potatoes, beans, lentils, millet, and peas. Of industrial
produce they grow flax and jute.

Lemkos are very poor today, since almost all their sources of earning money have dried up. Yet only fifty years ago [circa 1890] they
were well off. At that time, they not only raised animals, they sold
them as well. The Lemko Rusyns of Szepes, Sáros, and Zemplén
counties bought sheep every spring in Máramaros county, in
neighboring Bukovina, in Transylvania which belonged to Hungary,
and in Moldavia. The flocks were driven home where they grazed during the summer. This meant a two-fold profit. The poor soils were fer-
tilized by sheep manure. The sheep were sheared, cheese was made
from the milk, and the wool and the cheese were sold on domestic or
foreign markets. In the autumn, the sheep and the lambs were driven
to Hanušovce (Hanusfalu) in Sáros county or to Olomouc (Olmütz)
[in Moravia] and sold. At the Hanušovce market, merchants from
Austrian Bohemia, Moravia, and Silesia, as well as from German-
ruled Poznań (Posen) [now in Poland] came and paid high prices for
the fattened sheep. Some enterprising Lemkos even drove their sheep
to foreign markets year after year.

Some dealt in horses and cattle. The horses and the oxen were
bought in neighboring Bukovina, Poland, and Moldavia. The sales
continued until November when the pork business began, lasting from
mid-December until St. Paul's day (January 15). They stayed home
until April, and after the snow was gone they continued again the pattern mentioned above. Then, during the mid-nineteenth century, the
more economically mobile and talented Jews squeezed the Lemkos out
of the livestock market.

When a Lemko talks about the good old times, he is thinking of the
livestock market. "It was a great feast when flocks of sheep, herds of
oxen, and the studs arrived. They were dispersed to different grazing
lands. All the peasants, whether well to do or not, spent the night outdoors and took care of the animals. Merry songs could be heard, and
the bagpipe was played around the shepherd's bonfires. All this is no
longer the case," recalled with sadness the old shepherd of Osturna.
"If we want to survive, we have to go to America, but we cannot even
go there any more [i.e., 1939]."

The Lemkos, having an enterprising nature, went far away for their daily bread. A large number in Szepes county were door to door salesmen, peddlers, or repairmen. They travelled all over Austria-Hungary and sold edible oils, linens, butter, cheese, flasks, and other small items. A few had the gumption to go to foreign countries. They were liked in the southern part of the Russian Empire, in the God-forsaken small Ukrainian villages there. Later [at the turn of the twentieth century], the Russian government stopped them from coming because, it was said, they spread news about peasant revolts and other revolutionary movements.

Lemko repairmen (*drotary*) who fixed with zinc wire broken pottery and who put in new glass windowpanes to replace what was broken came from Rusyn villages in Szepes county. Usually a master and an apprentice wandered together, some with horse and buggy, others on foot carrying their supplies in a backpack. In some villages they stayed longer, replenishing their inventory, making various items from wire, and peddling their wares from house to house. They were merchants and craftsmen all in one. Those who fixed things with wire also made metal patches on damaged metal (usually cast iron) cooking utensils, and tied together pots with an intricately bent wire so that larger pottery vessels could be used to store grain or corn.

Except for wiring pots and replacing glass, the Lemkos seldom pursued other crafts. Although Lemkos were good weavers, linen-weaving remained a cottage industry for a long time in Szepes and Sáros counties. In older times, they could not engage in other crafts even if they had wanted, because all manufacturing was in German hands, and the Germans would not let others into their craftguilds. Moreover, craftsmen were city-dwellers, and Lemkos, like other Rusyns, had no towns or cities.

Physically, the Lemko had an even weaker body and was smaller than the Boiko. His face was thin and fallen in and could not be called attractive. His look was cold, inconsistent; his walk was lazy, uncertain. He was industrious and a great believer in God, but not as obliging as the Boiko. He was more egotistic than the other Rusyns, which was the result of his past experience in livestock raising and selling, and his life as a peddler in which he had to work for profit.

According to the manner in which they grasped ideas, and according to their way of thinking, customs, and in lifestyle, the Lemkos were closer to the West than either the Boikos or Hutsuls. This was understandable; after all, western peoples like the Magyars, Germans, Slovaks, and Poles surrounded the Lemkos, whose only contact with other Rusyns farther east was through a small corridor.

The Lemko was also closer in dress to the Slovak and the Pole than to his fellow highlander Rusyns. He did not wear a knife-holder, which was the pride of the Boiko and the Hutsul. Yet he wore a necktie, unknown to the Boikos. His traditional costume consisted of short wrinkled pants (*gatia*) and a shirt. Over the shirt he wore a vest studded with black sequins on top of which when outdoors he wore a long cassock with black and white fringes or, when at home, a tunic (*hunka*) reaching to the knee—the *serdak*. He did not wear a *kozhukh* [sheepskin vest]. The women dressed quite tastefully and were pretty. A blue or white kerchief was worn by married women, while unmarried girls did not wear anything on their heads. Skirts were mostly of a solid color. The poor Lemko went barefoot from spring to fall. In winter, he would wear shoes bought at the market or home-made shoes *bochkory*, and some have boots.

Like the other Rusyns, Lemkos sing while working and they have songs for both ceremonies and play. Lemkos also know many Magyar folksongs and many Magyar games in Rusyn translation. Hardly any old song is heard any more. In older songs the recurring theme is America. In general, Lemkos do not have many ancient tales or legends either. Perhaps the oldest event remembered by Lemkos—handed down from father to son—is the women's fair at Krásny Brod.

Until the beginning of the eighteenth century a market to arrange marriages was held once or twice a year in Krásny Brod in Zemplén county. This was the only women's fair among the Rusyns. Actually only Lemkos participated. Even if other Rusyns knew about it, they were unable to attend because of poor transportation facilities. It is strange that mention of the fair does not occur in folktales. In contrast, the Boikos and *Dolishniany* have older folktales.

At Krásny Brod, hundreds of families assembled around the Basilian monastery. The girls let down their hair and decorated it with flowers. Widows wore wreaths on their heads. The girls walked around and moved invitingly. The groom-candidates came also with parents and some relatives. This was the first time most boys and girls saw each other. When a boy found a girl that appealed to him, he stepped up to her, grasped her hand and said: "If you want a husband, here I am. Come to the priest." If the girl took to the boy, she kept on holding his hand. Then the girl led the boy to her family. After the boy agreed to the dowry, or purchase price of the girl, he led her family to his relatives and then all went into the monastery where a pious monk married them right away. He did not even ask the name of the groom and bride; neither was he interested in their home address. (Whether a marriage certificate was made or not, the legend does not reveal). After the ceremony, they ate, drank, and danced; then all went home. Frequently, this was the last time the parents saw their daughter and they often had no idea to whom she was married and in which village she would live.

Not all weddings were smooth events. Arguments and brawling were frequent. If a girl did not take to the boy and her parents defended her, but the boy insisted, the girl's male relative often attacked the suitor. A brawl started. At times, the girl might not like the boy, but because the boy offered a handsome dowry to the parents, they forced her to marry him. Abduction occurred too. If a young man saw that neither the girl nor her parents wanted him, at the appropriate moment he abducted the girl with the help of his relatives. He forced the girl to go to the monastery. For a good deal of money, a monk would marry them despite the protests of the girl.

Finally, the marriage fair ended in scandal. Abduction and brawling became more and more frequent. To the great sorrow of the Lemkos and to the even greater sorrow of the Basilians, after 1720 further purchases of brides were banned by the authorities.

CHAPTER SIX

Rusyn Culture and Literature

The Rusyns have no uniform spoken or literary language.[44] The reason may be that while some Rusyns were settled according to a plan, most had immigrated to Subcarpathia from different places and at various times. As a result they did not develop a common language until the present day, and before then it could not be raised to a literary language by Subcarpathian poets and writers. Instead, the poets and writers wasted their talent in barren arguments about language. And with sad results.

Before the end of the seventeenth century, we have no data about Subcarpathia's literature or its other cultural achievements: It is likely that the Subcarpathian Rusyns were not any more advanced than their brethren in the lands they left. In the thirteenth century, when their immigration to Hungary commenced, their religious rites resembled Eastern Orthodox Christianity. In practice, however, they followed the ancient Slavic pagan faith and did not adopt the spirit of Christianity. Russian church historians (Golubinskii, Makarii) proved that in the centuries following their conversion the common folk were not taught Christian doctrine and instead adopted only Byzantine Christian ceremonies. The priests were only concerned with following rigidly the formalities of the services, which they regarded as their only duty.

The Subcarpathian Rusyns could not have had any literature during their period of migration, because the life of the new settler was filled with breaking the virgin soil, clearing the forest, building homes, and establishing new villages. Throughout the Rusyns had to fight the forces of nature, while at the same time they found themselves in entirely new surroundings which they could not understand for a long time to come. The [Rusyn] serf of the Polish and Lithuanian landlord now became a serf of the Hungarian landowner. He had no idea of politics or social questions, because his time was filled entirely with a struggle to survive.

The earliest immigrants settled in those parts of Szepes and Sáros counties that were closest to the great Hungarian plains. They established villages by the end of the fifteenth and the beginning of the sixteenth centuries. As soon as they could afford it, they erected a small wooden church and set out to search for a priest. The first priests arrived from where the settlers originated or from where their ancestors came, in particular from Galicia. One or two priests brought with them ecclesiastical books written in Church Slavonic. Because too few books were available, they were copied in Subcarpathia. Due to oversight by such scribes, it was natural that one or two local language forms or expressions slipped into the text. This, however, did not constitute literature.

Our Rusyns had not and could not have had a literature until the end of the sixteenth century. While it is true that literature is a cultural necessity, immigrant Rusyn serfs had no cultural needs. Even today, shepherding and agricultural peoples in Europe, or in the Near and the Far East have no great desire for the printed word, for books, or for magazines. Similarly, seventeenth-century Rusyn society was composed of two elements, shepherds and peasants, and not even their spiritual leaders, the simple Orthodox priests, had cultural aspirations.

The often-mentioned and popular complaint of Rusyns that the Mongolo-Tatar invasion [1241], the Ottoman occupation [1524-1680], the Kuruc-Labanc War [eighteenth century], and other bloody upheavals destroyed the ancient Rusyn literary relics is plain nonsense. There was nothing to be obliterated. Ivan Franko, the prominent Ukrainian writer and literary historian proved this.

Subcarpathian Rusyn literature began through contacts with the West through Hungary. The Reformation and the union of the Orthodox Church with Rome were the two most important factors which led the Rusyn people of Subcarpathia toward the road of culturalization. [During the Reformation], Protestants came from Sáros and Zemplén counties and from Transylvania to Subcarpathia. With the support of landlords like Péter Perényi, Péter Petrovics, István Török and others, the Reformation gained momentum in Sátoraljaújhely, Sárospatak, and other towns, and eventually reached the Rusyns. The Protestant spirit took strongest root in Transylvania. Because Máramaros county belonged to Transylvania until 1733, the Mukachevo-Chynadiievo estate was for a long time in the hands of

Protestant princes who tried to convert the Rusyns to Protestantism. Although the Rusyns did not accept the Reformation, their horizons were widened as they were exposed to western ideas and thought. Sermons had been customary [along with the liturgy] in the Catholic Church before the Reformation. The Protestants more or less omitted the liturgy replacing it with teaching to explain the Gospel. To achieve their goals, Protestant clergy recited prayers in the language of the people and pronounced God's Word in the same vernacular tongue. The Orthodox adopted this custom from the Protestants, giving sermons and reciting prayers in the local language of the Rusyns.

The second event that greatly benefitted Rusyn culture was the church union with Rome in 1646. Seeing the intellectual backwardness of the Rusyns, Count György Drugeth, lord of the Humenné and Uzhhorod estates, entrusted the Greek Catholic bishop of Przemyśl [in Galicia], Atanasii Krupets'kyi (consecrated 1610, d. 1652), to unify with Rome. The Holy See of Rome approved of the idea, and the plan was put into the hands of the archbishop of Eger. After long negotiations, in 1646 the Rusyn clergy of the counties Szepes, Sáros, Zemplén, and Ung accepted the Union with Rome.

Farther east, the ruling princes of Transylvania did not permit the priests of Bereg and Máramaros counties to go to Uzhhorod. They wanted to convert them to Protestantism. Protestant leaders agitated against Catholicism in general, but mainly against the office of the Pope. The ruling princes of Transylvania succeeded in creating hatred [toward Catholics] in the hearts of the [Rusyn] Orthodox priests. Consequently, they attacked [fellow Rusyns] who were in union with Rome [the Uniates] in the harshest terms. As a result, Bereg and Máramaros counties unified with Rome only when they became separated from Transylvania.

By the second half of the seventeenth century, the Rusyns had become divided into two factions. Under Protestant influence, the eastern regions became Orthodox, while the western half became Greek Catholic (or Uniate) and under Roman Catholic influence. One would have expected extensive religious debates, which often stimulate intellectual life. However, things developed differently. Orthodox priests fiercely attacked the Roman and Greek Catholic clergy in their own churches and forbid their flock from speaking with them. All they wanted was to prevent their own followers from converting to Catholicism. They did not want to argue with the Catholic clergy. Therefore, the Catholics had no knowledge of their attacks and no debate followed.

Until the middle of the sixteenth century, a literate Rusyn's only intellectual nourishment consisted of liturgical books from Russia written in Church Slavonic. However, when the Rusyns became aware of western thinking and ideas under Catholic and Protestant influence, their priests needed more and better books.

As early as the end of the sixteenth century, the Rusyns who lived on the estates of Protestant Transylvanian princes demanded to be taught by their priests just as the Protestant clergymen were teaching their followers. Because the Orthodox priests were uneducated and ignorant, instructional books were needed. This was the beginning of the so-called Gospel commentaries, that is, sermons for Sundays and the Feasts of the year.

Orthodox Rusyn priests received the first Gospel commentaries from [Rus' lands in] Poland and re-edited them in their own language. During the rewriting, they also used Hungarian materials. In the process, editors adopted from the original source only what they liked, enlarging or abbreviating the material to fit their own knowledge and respond to their own level of scholarship. Local examples, folk tales, short stories, even superstitions were added. [The Rusyn editors] dealt arbitrarily not only with the commentaries but with the very text of the Gospel.

Every Orthodox priest prepared a book for himself in order to have something from which to deliver sermons. We should not, however, take the expression "sermon" literally. In effect, the priest read the sermon of the day, adding explanations from local life. Moreover, since almost every priest used the dialect of his own village to rewrite the sources, these works are characteristic of the savory folk-language which makes them very valuable from a literary point of view.

Unfortunately, and to the great loss of Rusyn literature, most of these manuscripts have disappeared. The Greek Catholic priests who took the place of the Orthodox and who were educated in a Latin culture, did not recognize the literary and linguistic value of the [local] manuscripts, which is perhaps understandable. Orthodox Bible commentaries first occurred in Subcarpathian literature during the seventeenth and eighteenth centuries, and so far some twelve to fifteen have been found and published by scholars.

The most interesting are the commentaries prepared by Orthodox priests in the lowland villages of the southwestern part of Máramaros county—Danylove (Sófalva), Uhlja (Uglya), Kolochava (Kalocsa), Njagovo (Nyágova, today Dobrians'ke)—interesting both for their content and language. The authors of these not only used the Galician Rusyn language, they also inserted Hungarian *postillas* or footnote-like explanations. While not much knowledge is revealed in these works, the fanaticism, faith, and unbroken adherence to their rite is unparalleled.

Frequently in the explanations, Greek philosophers like Aristotle, Plato, and Sophocles are mentioned, along with East Slavic saints and church fathers, even though nothing is known about them. For instance, before the names of Greek philosophers, the commentators often added the title "saint" or suggested that he was an important church father. The explanations are naive, on the level of folktales. All are consistently against Catholicism and in particular despise the church union and any association with Rome.

Even more popular than the scriptural commentaries were the *sbornyky*, or encyclopedic collective works. Their varied contents included sermons, apocryphal Biblical stories (apocrypha are books written by others using the name of Old Testament authors to achieve the authority of the Holy Scriptures), legends, folktales, fictional events, informative material from natural history, medicine, geography, astronomy, economics, and so forth. In the seventeenth and eighteenth centuries, many *sbornyky* changed hands. So far, researchers have published about ten. The favorite topics of the *sbornyky* were apocryphal Biblical stories. The Gospel, of course, did not include complete biographies. However, the common folk would want to know the whole life of their popular [biblical] heroes from the cradle to the grave, and apocryphal writings sought to satisfy their curiosity. Among the Slavs, it was a sect called Bogomils who first spread such writings. (The Bogomils or Bogumils were a sect that originated in Bulgaria in the tenth or eleventh century. Its followers believed in good and evil spirits. They did not eat meat and denied both the sacraments and priesthood). Bogomil books had found their way to Galicia in the thirteenth and fourteenth centuries and arrived in Subcarpathia by the end of the sixteenth century. Even today we can find one or two apocryphal stories in books used by the church. For instance, the stories of the ladder of Jacob, the vision of Isaiah, and the testament of the twelve patriarchs are all in the *Minea*—a book on the lives of saints which also contains songs praising the saints in the order of the calendar.

During the seventeenth and eighteenth centuries, Subcarpathia's

Orthodox priests preferred the apocryphal to the canonical books because they contained interesting stories which could hold their listeners spell-bound. There was hardly anybody among the Subcarpathian Rusyns who could read and write. This is why the *sbornyky* were edited for listeners, as is evident from an "advertisement" for the Uzhhorod *sbornyk*: "All who have ears—listen. Those who can write—write it down."[45] Orthodox priests read in church from the *sbornyky* and then loaned them for copying to those who could write.

Besides biographies of biblical figures, the people most liked to listen to accounts about the creation, the last judgment, life in the world beyond, the tortures of hell, death, and the Anti-Christ. Such tales were put together with the outlook of common people in mind. For instance, the story about the Last Judgment began: "When we appear before God's Holy Face, the king will stand behind the poor farmer, the officer behind the common soldier, the landlord behind his serf. Oh, how they will suffer when they have to go from the joys of earthly life into the realm of perpetual sadness."[46]

The Rusyn peasant and shepherd also received knowledge in natural sciences from the *sbornyky*. Thus, the Orthodox priest would read in the *sbornyky* how the lion is not only strong but clever too. When pursued, he obliterates his footsteps with his tail so nobody can find him. As for the eagle, it loses its eyesight when it gets old, but if it immerses itself three times in clear water—as true believers immerse the children in water at baptism—it regains its eyesight. The porcupine puts grapes and other berries on the top of his spikes and carries them to his children. Then there is a deer which lives a hundred years. It is the snake-eating deer. When it becomes fifty years old, it searches hills and valleys and looks into all animal dwelling places; and if it finds the snake's nest, it roars. First the deer smashes everything around him, then puts its nose on the stone under which the snake lives. When the snake emerges, the deer swallows it right away. If the snake does not want to come out, the deer carries water in his mouth, causing an inundation that forces the snake out. Then the deer rushes to the well to drink. If it drinks, it lives for 100 years exactly. If not, it soon dies. [Other natural phenomena] like thunder are explained as if the prophet Elijah is driving his carriage through heaven. The Rusyn peasant also has an explanation for earthquakes. The earth rests on three fishes. If one fish moves, the earth's crust over him will tremble also. From the *sbornyky*, the Rusyns also learned about the meaning of dreams, and in that context heard about the adventures of Alexander the Great. The Orthodox priests told them about the wonders of nature and the exploits of the Romans.

The information contained in the *sbornyky*, but moreso than the apocryphal tales, had a tremendous effect on the intellectual development of the Rusyns. Under the influence of apocryphal writings the popular religion of the masses and the Rusyn world view took shape. Even today [circa 1940] the Rusyn believes in superstitions and curses, and he has customs and legends which do not raise him much above the intellectual level of the eighteenth-century *sbornyky* copiers.

The copiers, editors, and rewriters of the *sbornyky* were driven by a desire to teach and enlighten their people. Therefore, they collected for this purpose all material that seemed to be worthwhile to know. This is why the content of the *sbornyky* is so varied. Nonetheless, the pious seventeenth- and eighteenth-century priests did not fail to point out that all the true knowledge they provided derived from God. It was the saints who told the people what is in the *sbornyky*. Thus, interpretations of dreams come from the prophet Daniel, while prayers against sickness were written down by St. Ambrosius. This is why even today many Rusyns think that their knowledge, customs, and even superstitions were handed down from the saints.

There are also some theological disputations from the seventeenth and eighteenth centuries. This is because some fanatical defenders of Orthodoxy were not satisfied to scold and abuse the Papists—Roman Catholics and Uniate Greek Catholics. To prove their point, they cited the Gospel, the writings of church fathers, and quotations from Hungarian polemics by Protestant theologians. Extremely interesting are the works of Mykhail Orosvyhove, who also used the pseudonym Mykhail Andrella or Mykhail Feodul. His main work carried a Latin title, *Tractatus contra Latinos et Graecocatholicos* (1672-81), although it is only the title of this three-volume manuscript which is in Latin.

Andrella was very familiar with the contemporary Hungarian religious polemics, but because he had no formal education and was not versed in rules of dialectic, he could not write a scientifically convincing work. Although he read a lot, he lacked the capacity of judgment. Andrella did use all the contemporary literature he could lay his hands on, and he quoted much of it. However, the main value of his writings is that they provide a primary source for contemporary thought.

Orosvyhove, alias Andrella, had great spirit and he was bold; yet, at the same time he was a narrow-minded fanatic. He stuck stubbornly to traditional customs and morals, and he obstinately believed that the Uniates had committed treason against Christ and Christianity.

The Orthodox priests (*bat'ky*) had no education; therefore, despite all their fanaticism, they could not stop the spread of church union. Nonetheless, for the longest time they were in a more favorable position than the Uniates. The majority of the people were with them; they had two prominent monasteries—one at Mukachevo and the other at Hrusheve (Körtvélyes); and the Protestant princes [in Transylvania] effectively supported them.

Allegedly, the monastery at Hrusheve had a printing shop. All Rusyn writers mention this, as do some books which were allegedly printed there. Even though all Rusyn writers state this, it is very unlikely that it is true. Nothing proves the existence of a printing shop and no one can produce a book which would indicate that it had been printed at Hrusheve. During the religious disputes, Orthodox priests urged their followers to write down whatever they heard about events regarding the church. Yet no such writings indicate the existence of a printing shop. In particular, Andrella's greatest desire was to make his writing available to the largest number of people, and if there had been a printing shop in the monastery at Hrusheve, it certainly would have been used by the defenders of Orthodoxy.

The poetry of the seventeenth and eighteenth centuries actually consisted only of religious songs. As a historical reference, the most important is a song entitled: "The Holy Pictures of Klokochov." This song tells about the siege of Vienna in 1683 and the liberation of Buda from the Turks in 1686. The unknown writer complained in the song that both the Kuruc and the Labanc destroyed everything. If Hungary is a good and a blessed place, its people are evil. They fight with each other and fight against the emperor of Vienna. The Turks were already driven out of Vienna, and Buda was liberated as well. Now the Turks are based in Belgrade (Nándorfehérvár). God grant that the Turks be driven out of Constantinople as well, acclaims the author happily. The author of the song is a Germanophile and he sees in the emperor the defender of Christianity.

The comparatively rich and varied popular literature of the seventeenth and eighteenth centuries remains in manuscript only. Its appearance came to an end at the end of the eighteenth century. None of these manuscripts, however, has any literary or scholarly value. For us [Magyars] they are valuable because the [Rusyn texts] are full of Hungarianisms.

In effect, the Rusyns adopted hundreds of Hungarian words into their language. In the oldest Subcarpathian text written in 1404,[47] we find the following Rusyn words: *urik* (from Hungarian *örök*: everlasting); *vitsishpan* (from *vicispán*: sheriff's assistant); *meshter*, as in the phrase, *Balitsa voievida i Drag meshter* (*mester*: master); *nemish* (from *nemes*: noble). The word *urik* still means in Rusyn: inheritance, but this sense of the word in Hungarian occurs in Hungarian-language texts only from the second quarter of the fifteenth century.

Many Hungarian words entered Rusyn with a changed meaning, and we can learn a lot from these. For example, the Hungarian *költség* means cost, but in its Rusyn form, *kelchik/kelchig*, it means food/foodstuff as in the sentence: *Poka budet kelchigu postnoho* (until we have fasting food).[48] Still today in some parts of Transylvania, the Hungarian word *költség* is used to designate "bread" or other food eaten with cornhash (*puliszka*); it may be "meat" or "cheese" or "cottage cheese." The Hungarian etymological dictionary lists several other uses of this meaning.

Most Hungarian words were adapted by Rusyns during the seventeenth and eighteenth centuries. Since many of the lowlander Rusyns (*Dolishniany*) spoke Hungarian, Orthodox priests often explained the meaning of some Slavic words and expressions using Hungarian words. Such explanations are found in examples of phrases from Rusyn texts with Hungarian explanations: *rod/nemzet* ("nation," in Rusyn and in Hungarian); *kotrym chinom/kipom* (meaning "by which," with *kipom* derived from the Hungarian *miképpen*); *iz chuzhoi zemli/orsaga* ("from a foreign country," with *ország* meaning country in Hungarian); *iz varosha/hrada* ("from the city" in both Hungarian and Rusyn, the former derived from the Hungarian word for city, *város*); *pred'il/khutar* ("boundary," with *khutar* derived from the Hungarian *határ*); *u temnytsiu/u rabshag upaly* ("they fell into captivity," with *rabshag* derived from the Hungarian *rabság*, meaning prison); *u chovni velykom/u gal'i* ("in a large boat," with *gal'i* derived from the Hungarian *gálya*); and from Andrella's writings the Rusyn/Hungarian juxtapositions: *izobral/valastoval* ("take away"), *skarb/kinch* ("treasure," with the latter form from the Hungarian *kincs*), and *kat/hovher* ("executioner," with the latter form from the Hungarian *hóhér*).[49] It often happened that a Rusyn writer or scribe explained how a Hungarian word is to be pronounced, as in: *zhona na imia Szuszana—a nashi suside zovut' ieiu Zhuzhana* (the woman's name is Suzana, but our Magyar neighbors say Zhuzhana).[50]

There are in Rusyn several expressions translated literally from Hungarian. Whooping cough (szamárköhögés) is in Rusyn *somarskij kashlei* (meaning: a donkey's cough), while in Ukrainian, it is *kashlyk* or *koklush*. The Hungarian word *pántlikás giliszta* (tasseled earthworm) becomes in Rusyn: *pantlykova hlista*, in Ukrainian: *hlysta, soliter*. The Hungarian: *én is úgy jártam* is in Rusyn: *ja takzhe tak khodyl* (I was going the same way), meaning: "it happened to me also." The Hungarian: *nótákat csináltak* is in Rusyn: *novty chynily* (they made songs, i.e., they were singing). The Hungarian *szerencsét próbálta* is in Rusyn: *serenchu probaloval* (They tried their luck). The Hungarian *szekéren megyek* (I am going by cart, i.e., I'll take a ride on a cart) is in Rusyn: *idu vozom* (I'll go on a cart).

We may assume that because of the Hungarian influence, Rusyns pronounce the so-called middle *l* sound, which does not occur either in Ukrainian, Polish, or Russian.[51] These languages know only a hard or soft *l*. Similarly, the labial sound of the *Dolishniany* was borrowed from Hungarian. Several Hungarian adverbs and conjunctions were adapted, such as: *pedig* (yet), *ugyan* (though), *dehogy* (by no means), *menten* (at once), *vagy* (or), *avagy* (either), *szinte* (almost). They are used in Rusyn in the same way as in Hungarian. The verbal prefix *yz/iz* is used just like the Hungarian *el* (from, away); for example, the Rusyn *izengeduval mu hrichi* (they took away his sins) is in Hungarian: *elengedte bűneit*. The Rusyns also adapted the typical introduction of Hungarian fairy tales. Thus, the Hungarian *Volt, hol nem volt* (It was, where it never was) becomes in Rusyn: *buv, de ne buv* or *byl, de ne byl*. The *Dolishniany* adapted as well the sudden changes and the refrains of Hungarian folksongs, such as *ihaj-csuhaj*; *kis angyalom* (my little angel) or *sárga recece* (yellow?). In short, the Hungarian spirit left a strong impact especially on the language and the thought pattern of the *Dolishniany*.

The popular literature of the seventeenth and eighteenth centuries indicates that the *Dolishniany* or lowlanders (i.e., the majority of Rusyns) spoke in those days the same way as they do today. Their language has not evolved much since then. This is because it was not cultivated in literary works. Had the development of the Rusyn language and literature not been artificially impeded, the Rusyns of our day would never tolerate being forced to learn Ukrainian or Russian.

The church union divided Rusyns into two factions. The western faction came under the jurisdiction of the Roman Catholic archbishopric at Eger, which was to have an intellectual and material influence upon the Rusyn clergy under its sway. At the time of the church union, the Greek Catholic clergy was as ignorant and uneducated as the Orthodox priests of Bereg and Máramaros counties. While no one thought of educating the Orthodox priests, the archbishop of Eger believed it was the duty of his archbishopric to train learned and reliable Greek Catholic priests. Because at the time the Eparchy of Mukachevo was very poor and with insufficient resources to maintain a seminary, arrangements were made soon after the union to send the candidates for the priesthood to Eger and Trnava (Nagyszombat). Following the request of the Mukachevo Bishop Petro Partenii (consecrated 1651, d. 1655), beginning in 1655 Emperor Ferdinand III (reigned 1639-1657) gave money for the education of [Greek Catholic] priests and cantors. Similarly in 1689, the county of Szepes allotted an annual sum of 300 florins for educational purposes, but this was still insufficient to support a seminary.

Bishop Joseph de Camillis (1689-1705) felt that a priest's education was an important and serious matter. Thus, for the use of theologians and priests he issued in 1698 a *Catechism* in Church Slavonic. This was the first printed book for the Subcarpathian Rusyns. However, the *Catechism* was too long and too difficult to understand. In any case, the priest's knowledge was often quite limited, and since they had trouble with reading and writing, they could barely understand the Catechism, let alone learn it. Realizing this difficulty, a year later de Camillis issued another book called a Primer (*Bukvar*), to which a small catechism was attached.

After de Camillis, the Mukachevo Bishop Gennadii Bizantii (1656-1733, consecrated 1716) made great efforts to raise the intellectual level of his priests. In 1727, he published in Church Slavonic *Kratkoe prypadkov moral'nŷkh yly nravnykh sobranie* (A Brief Collection of Moral Precepts). As a result, those candidates for the priesthood, who because of their inadequate primary education could not manage to attend Roman Catholic seminaries, studied instead from these three books. The bishop himself gave instruction and was helped by a few Uniate priests who had graduated from the Eger and Trnava seminaries.

Bishop Mykhail Ol'shavs'kyi (1700-1769, consecrated 1743) also did much to improve the education of Greek Catholic priests. At [a new] theological school at Mukachevo, he diligently instructed his pupils. The spirit of the times was Latin, so that only those persons who spoke Latin with perfection were regarded as educated. Ol'shavs'kyi, therefore, made several efforts to have the clergy learn Latin. In 1746, at Cluj (Kolozsvár), he published a book entitled

Elementa puerilis institutionis in lingua latina (The Basic Principles of the Latin Language for Youth), and under each Latin word in the text the meaning was given in Rusyn and Church Slavonic.

Nonetheless, these efforts were still inadequate, so that finally, upon the urging of the bishop of Mukachevo, in 1776, Empress Maria Theresa founded a seminary at Uzhhorod—the Seminarium Regioepiscopale Diocaesanum. In the beginning, the language of teaching was both Latin and Church Slavonic. In 1809, however, they switched entirely to Latin, with only one or two subjects still taught in Rusyn and later in Hungarian. Some promising Greek Catholic priests [from the Mukachevo Eparchy] continued their studies in Rome, either at the Athanaseum, or later in the Collegium Ruthenicum, founded in 1886 by Pope Leo XIII (reigned 1878-1903). Some studied in Trnava or in Eger, in Vienna at the Barbareum, or the Pazmaneum in Budapest. Some also studied in Esztergom and in Budapest. However, the majority of Greek Catholic priests graduated from the Uzhhorod seminary, which always had the same high level of education as the other Roman Catholic seminaries in the Hungarian Kingdom. As for cantors (the *diaky*, who also served as village elementary school teachers), they were educated at the Cantor-Teacher's College in Uzhhorod.

Ever so slowly the Greek Catholic priests became better educated during the time of Bishop Ol'shavs'kyi. They learned Latin and tried to speak that language not only among themselves but also within their families. As a result, by the end of the eighteenth century, young men who prepared for the priesthood—usually sons of priest—knew very little Rusyn. This situation was described in a circular letter of Bishop Bachyns'kyi dated September 4, 1798: "I notice with deep sorrow that sons of Rusyn parents, after spending many years in Latin schools, apply to the seminary to become priests and are so ignorant and not versed at all in Rusyn that they can neither read nor write their own names in this language. They cannot even open their mouths in [Rusyn] church singing, let alone talk about church rites."[52]

Hence, the educated, yet latinized Greek Catholic clergy seemed to drift away from their own people. In those sections of Bereg and Máramaros counties which had become Greek Catholic, the common people who used to get their knowledge from the encyclopedic *sbornyky* and who used to think in an eastern fashion now received educated, westernized priests whom they could not understand. In the past, the Orthodox priests had wanted to educate their people and edited *sbornyky* for them. Now, the people did not even get those books. Instead, the Greek Catholic priests wrote in Latin, which reflected the spirit of the times [throughout Europe]. Nonetheless, the activity of the latinized Greek Catholic priests eventually had a positive effect on the masses, who through sermons and personal contact learned much more from them than from the naive Orthodox priests of times past.

For example, the provincial-general of the Order of St. Basil, Ioanniky Bazylovych, wrote his great two-volume historical work in Latin: *Brevis notitia fundationis Theodori Koriatovich* (Košice, 1799-1807). In this work, he hoped that in the interests of his monastery in Mukachevo he could prove the validity of the forged Koriatovych foundation document.

Similarly, the deacon of Uzhhorod, Mykhail Pop-Luchkai (1798-1848), wrote his works in Latin and Church Slavonic. His main work, *Historia Carpatho-Ruthenorum* (A History of the Carpathian Rusyns) exists in manuscript only.[ii] The dean of Chynadiieve (Beregszentmiklós), Ivan Dulishkovych (1815-1883), translated and re-edited this manuscript into Russian between 1874 and 1877. Luchkai's other important work, *Grammatica Slavo-Ruthena* (A Slaveno-Rusyn Grammar), was published in Buda in 1830, and for its time is quite a good book. The author knew the language of his own village Velyki Luchky (Lucska) very well. Then, in 1831, he published his sermons in two volumes, written in a mixed Rusyn and Church Slavonic language. Until the end of the nineteenth century, some priests still used Luchkai's sermons.

Right up until the late nineteenth century, the Rusyn clergy had only three books in Church Slavonic, the two catechisms of de Camillis, and the catechism of Bizantii. No book had been prepared for the common folk. Hence the aim of Canon Ivan Kutka (d. 1812) was to fill this lacuna. In 1803, he published in Buda a *Catechism* for public schools, but the language—basically Church Slavonic to which some Rusyn and Russian words were added—was artificial and too difficult. The construction of sentences was borrowed partly from Church Slavonic and partly from Latin. For children in the villages it was virtually incomprehensible. Nevertheless, it was used until the end

---

ii. Recently, Luchkai's *Historia* has finally begun to be published in the Latin original with parallel translation into Ukrainian. Volumes I and II have already appeared in *Naukovyi zbirnyk Muzeiu ukraïns'koï kul'tury u Svydnyku*, XI, XIII, XIV (Svidník, Bratislava, and Prešov, 1983-88), pp. 45-79, 109-245, 93-258.

of the nineteenth century, and village folk eventually got quite accustomed to it.

A typical representative of [Rusyn] national rebirth was Vasilii Dovhovych (1783-1849), a parish priest at Velyki Luchky, later Mukachevo, and finally Khust. He was also a corresponding member of the Hungarian Academy of Sciences. As a student, Dovhovych wrote poetry in Latin only. Upon finishing his formal education, he wrote first in Latin, later in Rusyn, then in Hungarian. Toward the end of his life, he wrote in Hungarian only. His Hungarian writings were published. Of his Rusyn writings, only his catechism in verse form was printed as an appendix to Kutka's *Catechism*.[jj] Some of his Rusyn poems also appeared in Luchkai's *Grammatica Slavo-Ruthenorum* (1830), while Dovhovych's other Rusyn works, the *Small, Middle, and Large Catechisms*, remained in manuscript only.

The majority of the Rusyn intelligentsia pursued the same path as Dovhovych. Unfortunately, and to the detriment of the people, a number of [intellectual leaders] became victims of Panslavism. Under the influence of the teachings of Jan Kollár (1793-1852),[kk] those few teachers and intellectuals who felt a sense of belonging with the great mass of Slavic people rejected Rusyn as a language and began to promote the idea of Muscovite-Russian linguistic unity. According to Kollár's brand of Panslavism, it is the destiny of small Slavic peoples to amalgamate with the larger Slavic nations to which they are related. For example, the Slovaks should become Czechs and the Rusyns and Ukrainians should become Russian. Among the Rusyns, it was their leaders Adol'f Dobrians'kyi (1817-1901) and Ivan Rakovs'kyi (1815-1885), who instilled in them a sense of Russophilism. They convinced a segment of the Rusyn clergy to believe that the Russian language was their language and that Russian literature was their literature.

Meanwhile, the educated Greek Catholic clergy was not at all aware of Rusyn folk literature from the seventeenth and eighteenth cen-

---

jj. Recently, a major collection of Dovhovych's poetry has appeared with facsimile reproduction of the original manuscript and translation into Ukrainian:"Poëmata Basilii Dohovits/Rukopys Vasylia Dovhovycha (1832)," *Naukovyi zbirnyk Muzeiu ukraïns'koï kul'tury u Svydnyku*, X (Svidník, Bratislava, and Prešov, 1982), pp. 111-232.

kk. Jan Kollár was a Slovak writer whose best known work propounding the unity and future glory of the Slavs is the epic poem *Slavy dcera* (The Daughter of Slavia, 1832).

turies. They knew nothing of the scriptural commentaries, nor did they read the *sbornyky* or religious polemics. Yet, even if they had heard of them, they probably would not have cared, because they were poorly written, were regarded as heretical, and were looked down upon because of their "peasant style."

Next to Dobrians'kyi, Ivan Rakovs'kyi was the most significant promoter of Russophilism. He was the editor of *Tserkovnaia gazeta* [Budapest, 1856-58], a newspaper published by the St. Stephen Society. It was the first organ intended for the Rusyn clergy. However, the publication was short-lived, because of the Muscovite Russian language it used that Rusyn readers did not understand. Already in the second quarter of its first year of publication, 140 of the *Tserkovnaia gazeta's* 390 subscribers returned it complaining they would only accept a paper they could understand. Despite the collapse of the *Tserkovnaia gazeta*, Rakovs'kyi continued to experiment. His new enterprise was the *Tserkovnyi viestnik* [Budapest, 1858], which due to lack of subscribers lasted for only ten issues. This paper also was printed in standard Russian. In fact, Rakovs'kyi was so concerned about maintaining the purity of the [Russian] language that he even asked Voitkovskii, [the Russian Orthodox] priest of Üröm, to correct his articles. It was because of the influence of Dobrans'kyi and Rakovs'kyi that Aleksander Dukhnovych, who started out and was considered the greatest Rusyn national poet, became a promoter of the Russian language and literature.

Dukhnovych was born on April 24, 1803, in Topol'a (Topolya) in the county of Zemplén, attended *gymnasia* in Uzhhorod and Košice, and completed his theological studies in Uzhhorod. He worked for three years in the office of the eparchy in Uzhhorod, then became tutor for the children of Petrovay, the vice-lieutenant of Uzhhorod, from 1830 until 1833, when he was named to the parish at Chmel'ova (Komlósa). In 1834, he became the parish priest in Beloveža, a post at which he remained until 1838. Then he went to Uzhhorod to become the eparchial consistorial notary. In 1844, he returned to Prešov Eparchy where he was promoted to canon. Because of Dukhnovych, Prešov was to become the center of intellectual life in Subcarpathian Rus'. In 1850, he founded at Prešov a literary society, which he subsequently reorganized in 1862, renaming it the St. John the Baptist Society. He died March 30, 1865.

Dukhnovych was extremely fond of his people—those God-fearing, clean-hearted, honest Rusyns. It pained him that they were backward in cultural matters. The reason for this, he thought, was the lack of public schooling and the non-existence of educational publications. Perhaps this was the reason why his first book carried the title, *Knyzhytsa chytalnaia dlia nachynaiushchykh* (A Reader for Beginners [Buda, 1847]). With its richness and versatility, it surpassed similar books written in other languages. It was written in Rusyn with some Church Slavonic elements interspersed in the text. Youngsters understood and liked to read it. To help in distributing this book, Dukhnovych gave to students 2000 copies gratis. Dukhnovych later wrote a book to be used by teachers: *Kratkii zemlepys dlia molodŷkh rusynov* (A Brief World Georgraphy for Young Rusyns, 1851). In his book, he wrote how Rusyns were "good hearted, musical, and appreciative of science and art, but because of unfortunate circumstances they were a poor and downtrodden people who deserve to be helped right away."[53] His prayer book, *Khlîb dushy* (The Bread of the Soul, 1851) had great success. Dukhnovych also wrote the first Rusyn play, "Dobrodîtel' prevyshaet bohatstvo" ("Virtue Is More Important than Riches," 1850). Although aesthetically weak, with no spiritual message and lifeless dialogues, Rusyns have performed this play with pleasure even to this day [1940], because they can understand it. Dukhnovych tried his hand at history as well, but because he was unacquainted with historical documentation, his *Istinnaia istoriia Karpato Rossov ili Ugorskikh Rusinov* (A True History of the Carpatho-Russians or Hungarian Rusyns, 1853) is a naive tale about the glorious past of the Rusyns.[ll]

Rusyns remember Dukhnovych most for his poetry. Actually, poetry was his weakest side and he was unable to create a good form. While its contents are not without fault, he is best remembered for [a text that was to become] the national anthem of the Rusyns:

> Subcarpathian Rusyns,
> Arise from your deep slumber!
> The voice of the people is calling you—
> Don't forget your own!
> Our beloved people,
> Let them be free,
> Let them be spared of

---

ll. Although completed in 1853, this work was not published until 1914 when a Russian translation by Fedir F. Aristov appeared in *Russkii arkhiv,* LII, 4-5 (Moscow, 1914), pp. 529-559. It was subsequently reprinted in O.V. Dukhovych, *Tvory,* Vol. II (Bratislava and Prešov, 1967), pp. 531-566 and translated by Iuliian Kolesarov into Vojvodinian Rusyn (Montreal, 1981).

Hostile storms.
Let justice be implanted
Among the whole Rusyn race!
The desires of the Rusyn leaders:
Long live the Rusyn people!
We all pray to the Lord on high
To preserve and give us a better Rusyn life.[54]
Another poem which the Rusyns also consider their national anthem, begins with these lines:
I was, am, and will remain a Rusyn.
I was born a Rusyn.[55]

Then, for the next forty lines he explains how all in his family were Rusyns and why he remained so. Despite its naïveté and primitiveness, the poem had a tremendous impact. It is the only poem from the nineteenth century in which a Rusyn poet delivers an open testimony about his nationality. There is hardly any true Rusyn who does not know it.

Some of Dukhnovych's popular songs reveal his talent. He probably would have been able to produce artistic work if the Russophiles had not diverted his attention from his own people's language and culture. Even so, his greatest merit was to spread Rusyn culture and literature. He shook the Subcarpathian intelligentsia and challenged them to take an interest in their own people and in their language. He was to the Rusyns what Kazinczy was to Hungarians.[mm] He sacrificed all his free time and all his efforts for the preservation of Rusyn culture. He issued almanacs and calendars, and he urged his contemporaries to learn Rusyn. Later, unfortunately, all his attempts to urge them to learn Russian and to read and write in that language were a waste of effort.

It is unfortunate that Dukhnovych's friends, who were Russians at heart, turned him away from the right path. Even so, when he was still writing at the beginning of his career poetry and prose in Rusyn, not Russian, he proved that one could write adequately in the vernacular Rusyn of Subcarpathia, in the same way the simple Orthodox priests had done in the seventeenth and eighteenth centuries. As long as he remained on familiar home ground, he achieved rather remarkable and

---

mm. Ferenc Kazinczy (1759-1831) was Hungary's greatest writer and literary organizer during the period of classicism. His own writings and translations contributed to making modern Hungarian suitable as a literary language.

valuable work. But his inclination toward Russophilism killed both the poet and writer in him.

In 1865, the Society of St. Basil the Great was founded with great enthusiasm upon the initiative of Dukhnovych. The aim of the society was to publish newspapers, books, and other literature in order to raise the cultural standards of the people. However, the initial enthusiasm proved to be only a flicker, because the society soon fell under the leadership of Russophiles. In fact, Dobrians'kyi, Rakovs'kyi, Viktor Kimak, Kyril Sabov, and Aleksander Mitrak were the leaders who decided its fate right from the beginning.

Two years after its formation, the Society published a few textbooks in the Russian language and in the same year began to issue the newspaper *Svît* [Uzhhorod, 1867-71]. In issues 4 and 7 of *Svît*, the program of the St. Basil Society was outlined. Among other comments, the programmatic statement read: "We don't even have to talk about literature. We have a ready-made, developed literature; only it has so far not become widely known. We do not have to create literature as our Magyar brothers did; all we have to do is learn it. Our task is a hundred times easier than that of our compatriots and brothers mentioned above. . . . We must strive to learn the ready-made Russian literature." In effect, the St. Basil Society was trying to transplant to Subcarpathia a literature which was strange in both language and spirit. It could be understood neither by the ordinary folk nor by the intelligentsia.

When it began publication, *Svît* had 410 subscribers. By the end of its first year, however, subscriptions declined to half that number, because the readers did not understand the Russian language. Many subscribers even complained about this in letters to the editor, of which a few were published. In the first number of 1868, one reader wrote: "I was thinking about the reasons why our newspaper has declined. I consulted others too. Now I can voice an opinion: it is both mine and that of the public. The readers think the main reason for the decline of *Svît* is its language. They say *Svît* is written in a language that no one understands. Apparently, the members of the editorial staff take words, idioms, and sayings from dictionaries. They do not use the language we speak and do not use expressions we know, that which every reader would understand without the use of a dictionary. Readers demand that you write in our language, without fancy words, Russian idioms, and new expressions. It is a pity to spend two forints a year on something one cannot understand."[56]

The editors of *Svît* did not change, and more and more readers returned the newspaper, cancelling their subscriptions. Finally, in 1869, it was decided that instead of using the Russian literary language it would be preferable to create a language composed of Church Slavonic (in its Russian version), Russian, and local Rusyn vocabulary. Even though no one wanted such an unwieldy creation, the Society nonetheless experimented with this artificial medium until 1871, at which time *Novỹi svît* [Uzhhorod, 1871-72] began to appear. After almost two years, it failed for the same reason as had *Svît*. Between 1872 and 1886, Canon Nikolai Homichko (1833-1886) published *Karpat*, a small-sized newspaper which had limited success. After *Karpat* folded, Ievhenii Fentsik printed at his own cost *Listok* [Uzhhorod, 1885-1903], until his own death in 1903. *Listok* was written in language that was a mixture of Subcarpathian Rusyn, Church Slavonic, and Russian. In the first issue, Fentsik wrote: "In my opinion, our journal which starts today, should be in Russian, should use the Russian language. Our language is the generally accepted Russian literary tongue which developed from Church Slavonic. We want to avoid misunderstanding and trouble in this respect. Our aim is to build and educate, not to cause disturbance or ruination."[57]

In his journal, Fentsik tried to publicize Slavic literatures and the life of Slavic people in general. He also ran language lessons in Russian. Beginning in 1891, a supplement for the common folk was appended to *Listok*, but it had hardly any readers. First of all, the supplement was written in a language no one could understand; secondly, only moralising and religious articles were published, and not many cared for this. It is interesting to note that shortly before his death Fentsik explained once more what he had indicated at *Listok's* inception: "Our aim is to draw our Hungarian-Russian language closer to literary Russian. This is rather important, because as we get closer and closer to Ukrainophilism along with it goes infidelity."[58]

Besides Rakovs'kyi and Dobrians'kyi, other writers associated with the St. Basil Society included Aleksander Mitrak, Iulii Stavrovs'kyi-Popradov, Evmenii Sabov, and Nikolai Homichko. With the exception of Dobrians'kyi, all were Greek Catholic priests; therefore, Subcarpathia's Russophile literature in the nineteenth century was didactic and religious in character.

Adol'f Dobrians'kyi (1817-1901) was one of the organizers of the 1848 Slav Congress [in Prague]. At the congress, he proposed to unite the Rusyn populated areas of the Austro-Hungarian monarchy—that is, Subcarpathian Rus', Galicia, and Bukovina—into an independent political unit. After the outbreak of the [1848 Hungarian] revolution,

Dobrians'kyi fled to L'viv (Lemberg), where he joined the "Carpatho-Russian" council, appointing himself representative of the "Carpathian Russians."[nn] By 1849, the Austrian government was most concerned about the revolution in Hungary, and it called upon the tsar of Russia for help. Dobrians'kyi was then appointed by the Austrian government as commissioner to aid the Russian troops. Thus, Dobrians'kyi returned to Hungary with Russian forces, as a Muscovite leader. After the Hungarian revolution was suppressed, the Austrian government appointed Dobrians'kyi lieutenant-governor of the four Rusyn-inhabited counties of Subcarpathia. He made every effort to Russianize the Rusyns, and when he could not achieve anything he left his government job and spent the rest of his time trying to organize the Rusyns. In 1881, he moved to L'viv and from there to Innsbruck [in the farwestern Austrian half of the empire] where he died in 1901.

Dobrians'kyi wrote a lot in Russian, but his writings have dubious value and should be regarded more as propaganda. With a florid imagination, he produced a map which indicated the western border of "Carpathian Russia" at the time of Saint Vladimir, ruling grand prince of Kievan Rus' between 980 and 1015. However, this area had never belonged to the principality of Kiev and at that time not a single Rusyn lived in Subcarpathia. Dobrians'kyi also forged historical documents on purpose in order to prove that there was a *Marchia Ruthenorum* (supposedly synonymous with Subcarpathian Rus') and a *Rus'ka Kraina*. For instance, he cited a document dated 1248 stating: *In Russia sub magna porta Galicia, que vocatur Ungarica.*[59] This means: "In Rus' below the great gate of Galicia which is called Hungary." Anyone who knows Latin realizes that in this sentence the attribute *Ungarica* (Hungary) refers to the word *porta* (gate). Dobrians'kyi, however, simply omitted the words *sub magna porta Galicia* and quoted only *in Russia Ungarica*. With similar imagination and distorted quotations Dobrians'kyi wrote about the "old [Orthodox] faith" (*stara vira*), about political conditions of the Rusyns,

---

nn. The body in L'viv was actually called the Holovna Rus'ka Rada (Supreme Rusyn Council), which from its establishment in May 1848 strove to obtain political and cultural rights for all Rusyns living in the Austro-Hungarian Empire. Dobrians'kyi was received enthusiastically by the Supreme Rusyn Council on April 20, 1849, and as a result that body addressed a petition to the emperor calling for the union of Subcarpathian Rusyns with their Galician and Bukovinian brethren.

and about other problems. He was the first chairman of the St. Basil Society and he took an active part in its direction.

Ivan Rakovs'kyi (1815-1885) was professor at the Uzhhorod Teacher's College. Later, between 1850 and 1859, he was an official government translator. But, instead of translating governmental statutes and acts of parliament into Rusyn, he translated them into Muscovite Russian. During his stay in Budapest, he was the editor of the *Tserkovnyi viestnik* and *Tserkovnaia gazeta*, which were printed in Russian. As vice-chairman of the St. Basil Society, he was the right hand man of Dobrians'kyi. Rakovs'kyi wrote several textbooks, all in Russian, and to make it possible for the Rusyns to learn Russian, he published [in Hungarian] *Orosz nyelvtan* (A Russian Grammar, Uzhhorod, 1867). From 1859 until his death, he was the parish priest in Iza (Máramaros county). Many attribute to Rakovs'kyi's activity the importance of Iza for Panslavic activities before World War I.[oo]

Aleksander Pavlovych (1819-1900), a parish priest in Vyšni Svidnik (Felsővizköz) published his writings in several Subcarpathian newspapers. He wrote moralizing, religious, and sermon-like poetry for the annual Rusyn almanac in Uzhhorod and also for the newspapers *Slovo* and *Zoria halytskaia* in L'viv.

An even more interesting literary career was that of Anatolii Kralyts'kyi (1834-1893), archimandrite at the Basilian monastery of Mukachevo. He was the only nineteenth-century Subcarpathian writer to draw consistently on topics from the life of the people. However, since his articles were published in the journal *Besieda* in L'viv, they never had any impact because the Subcarpathian Rusyns never read them. Kralyts'kyi also collected and published Rusyn linguistic remnants that were adopted into Hungarian. On the other hand, he did not hesitate to forge source material if he felt it was in the interest of his people and the monastery he headed. For instance, he was the author of the so-called, "Chronicle of Mukachevo," allegedly dating from the year 1458. A typical example of his forgeries is the "historic" tale, "Kniaz Laborets'" (Prince Laborets'). No doubt Kralyts'kyi had good intentions, and he could have created serious and valuable literary work if Russophilism had not pushed him off the

---

oo. Not long after Rakovs'kyi's death, Iza became in 1902 the first Subcarpathian village to "return" to the Orthodox faith. It was also from this village that the leading defendants came who were placed on trial for treason at Marmarosh Sighet in 1913.

right track. He, too, was a victim of the influence of Dobrians'kyi and Rakovs'kyi.

Ievhenii Fentsik (1844-1903) wrote poetry using the pen-name Vladimir. He was a poet, critic, editor, and storyteller all in one. His works were written in a language that was a composite of Church Slavonic and Russian, and they were published in *Slovo* in L'viv and later in the newspapers of the St. Basil Society [in Uzhhorod], *Svît* and *Karpat*. After these publications ceased to print his writing, he started at his own cost the journal *Listok*, which appeared every two weeks. He also published several prayer books and textbooks and wrote the first Subcarpathian novel, *Votchynî bez otechestva* (In the Land of My Birth Without a Homeland), which came out at the end of the 1870s. It is interesting to note that in 1878, at a festival of the Slavic Charity Club in St. Petersburg, Professor O.F. Miller read sections from this novel to prove that outside the territory of Russia there were "Russian" authors, although Miller did not mention the author's name. Fentsik was the author of the greatest [Rusyn] epic poem of the nineteenth century, the dramatic work, "Koriatovych." The full extent of Fentsik's imagination was evident in both his novel and epic poem in which the historical background was deliberately forged. Fentsik translated several Slavic authors as well. The basic characteristics of his writings are a deep religiosity, idealism, Slavic melancholy, and Russophilism.

Ivan Sil'vai (1838-1904) wrote under the pseudonym Uriel Meteor. He favored use of the Russian language, even though he did not know Russian well. Thus, he wrote in an artificial Russian language sprinkled with words that he invented. Sil'vai came from a Rusynized old Hungarian noble family. For his themes, he drew from the good old days when folk-singers, troubadours, and wandering minstrels visited royal courts and castles of the Hungarian nobility. Sil'vai wrote both short stories and poetry. His prose reveals elements of a vivid imagination and he dealt with social problems as well. On the other hand, his poetry borrowed themes from the Apocrypha, such as the story of "Enoch and Hosea, the Tree of Life". Sil'vai was the most productive [Rusyn] author of the nineteenth century. Nonetheless his output was barren, and as one of his critics remarked, "he competely neglected his times and his people."[60]

In his most fascinating autobiography, Sil'vai stated among other things that Russophilism is an artificial orientation without roots in our homeland. Moreover, he admitted honestly that he understood no Russian in his twenties, and that he still understood hardly a word of that language when he was sixty. When he wrote, he composed his sentences first in Hungarian, then translated them into Russian, always realizing that the result was weak. He had no idea at all about stress [in Russian]. During his theological studies in Budapest, Rakovs'kyi came in every day to teach Russian to Rusyn theology students. "We had no dictionary, nor grammar," wrote Sil'vai. "I studied the Slavonic Bible published in the time of Tarkovych [the early nineteenth century] and read it from the beginning to the end. With the help of the Latin Vulgate [edition of the Bible], I figured out the meaning of words and expressions." Nonetheless, Sil'vai expressed indignation in his autobiography toward those "who still believe that the language of the common people, such as peasants and laborers, can form a foundation for literature."[61]

Aleksander Mitrak (1837-1913) was a parish priest who wrote poetry, prose, and compiled a dictionary. At the beginning of his literary career he felt he was Hungarian, but then admitted in his poem, "My Awakening," that like Sil'vai, Rakovs'kyi had won him over to Russophilism. For poetry Mitrak used the pen-name Materin. After Rakovs'kyi published his Russian grammar for Rusyns to learn that language, he urged his good friend Mitrak to compile a dictionary. Therefore, in 1881 Mitrak published in Uzhhorod at his own expense a *Russko-mad'iarskii slovar* (*Russian-Hungarian Dictionary*), 3,000 copies of which he donated to the St. Basil Society to be distributed at low prices. His *Madiarsko-russkii slovar'* (*Hungarian-Russian Dictionary*) was published only in 1932.

Iulii Stavrovs'kyi-Popradov (1850-1899), a Greek Catholic parish priest in Čertižné, (Csertesz), was directly influenced by Dobrians'kyi. At Dobrians'kyi's country house in Čertižné, it was not uncommon to find Slavic scholars and politicians from foreign countries who would be visiting. At such occasions, Stavrovs'kyi-Popradov was also invited. Stavrovs'kyi wrote in a language that was simpler and easier to understand than that of Fentsik, Sil'vai, or Mitrak. He was well read, although his poems are often artificially over sentimental.

Evmenii Sabov (1859-1934) taught Rusyn in the Uzhhorod *gymnasium* [secondary school]. Later, he became the parish priest in Sevliush, and finally, archdeacon of the county of Ugocsa. He gained fame with his critical essays. His main work, *Khristomatiia tserkovno-slavianskikh i ugro-russkikh literaturnykh pamiatnikov* (An Anthology of Church Slavonic and Hungarian-Russian Literary Monuments, [Uzhhorod, 1893]), was for a long time the only literary history of the Subcarpathian Rusyns and it is still a very valuable work. During the Czech occupation, Sabov served as president of the Dukhnovych Society until his death in 1934.

Subcarpathian literature of the nineteenth century was basically no more than the part-time activity of a few writers who knew more or less the Russian language. However, it was neither read by the local intelligentsia nor by the Rusyn masses. As a result, neither Russian literature nor Rusyn writers got what they deserved. Before anyone even noticed them, they were forgotten, and today at best they remain on the yellowing pages of newspapers and almanacs. At times, their sleep [on those pages] is disturbed by scholars, but only curiosity moves them since they could not be seeking any literary treasures.

Some linguists, who during the Czech occupation had too much time on their hands, dug up from their quiet resting place a few works of those "Carpathian Russian" writers and even published some volumes. At best, however, these have only bibliographical value, because whoever wants to read Russian writers will not make any effort to read Fentsik, Sil'vai, Mitrak, Kralyts'kyi, or their companions. During the nineteenth century, there was no connection between the Rusyn people and Russian literature written in Subcarpathian Rus'. Furthermore, one reason for the much acclaimed backwardness of the Rusyn folk was precisely the fact that they could not understand and therefore did not bother to read works written in the artificial Carpathian or the literary Russian language.

In order to raise the cultural level of the Rusyns and put an end to this impossible situation, the Hungarian government decided to intervene. In 1881, it commissioned Vasylii Chopei to prepare Rusyn school texts. Chopei's language was close to that spoken by Rusyns, and as a result his books were easily understood and well read. Their only shortcoming was that they were written in a true western spirit, which was strange to Rusyns who had been reared in an eastern cultural environment. Chopei translated almost word for word the Hungarian school books of János Gáspár. Most unfortunate was the fact that Chopei omitted texts that would have been close to the Rusyn soul. It is interesting to note that Fentsik, Sil'vai, and a few other writers protested against Chopei's "ruining the language," and this created great difficulties in the implementation of educational reforms being attempted in Subcarpathian Rus'. From 1898 to 1919, the Hungarian government also published a weekly for village people called *Nedîlia*, which appeared in an understandable and clear Rusyn language. Then, beginning in 1896, it published in Uzhhorod a Rusyn journal called *Nauka*.

Toward the end of the nineteenth century, a few well-educated Rusyns were concerned about the cultural backwardness of their people, and they wished to educate the masses. They tried to communicate with the people in the Rusyn vernacular such as it was spoken in Subcarpathia. Among them was the very productive Iurii Zhatkovych (1855-1920), a Greek Catholic priest in Stroine (Malmos). Although his more valuable historical essays appeared in Hungarian, he also wrote some short stories in Rusyn as spoken in his village.

Another of these intellectuals was Avhustyn Voloshyn (1874-1945), who was also the editor of *Nauka* for a while. He wrote several popular stories and an excellent grammar (1907). However, during Czech rule, he developed political ambitions which diverted him from his original interests—to educate the people. This turned him as well toward Ukrainophilism, an orientation which is basically alien to our Rusyns.

The period of Czech occupation

Until the end of the nineteenth century and actually down to World War I, Subcarpathian writers were with one or two exceptions all priests. Not surprisingly, a religious spirit is predominant in that literature. But the character of literary output changed after the war as secular writers replaced clerical ones.

Between pre- and post-war Subcarpathian literature, there is no connection. A new life started after the Czech occupation, and while the Rusyns suffered, they did not play an active role in intellectual pursuits. Many Russian and Ukrainian refugees from the war and revolution sought and found a new home in Subcarpathian Rus'. The Russians promoted the Russian and the Ukrainians a Ukrainian language orientation. Driven by opportunistic motives, some Rusyns joined the Russian movement, some the Ukrainian orientation, while the majority favored a local orientation. The Rusyns who belonged to the Prosvita Society [a pro-Ukrainian cultural society] declared that their language and literature was identical with Ukrainian. On the other hand, members of the Dukhnovych Society [a pro-Russian cultural society] fought for the Russian language and literature. Yet, there were also followers of another trend—those who cultivated [a distinct] Subcarpathian language and literature. However, the Czechs did not sympathize with them. Those Rusyns who defended the cause of the Rusyn common man knew that the Rusyn folk language, in the form in which it was developed by Orthodox priests in the seventeenth and eighteenth centuries and which remained in manuscript, was suitable to express not only concrete but also abstract ideas as well. They knew that the Rusyns did not have to borrow from other languages.

The "classical" [Subcarpathian] Russian writers in the nineteenth century despised the Rusyn language and literature, which could only survive on the lips of the ordinary people. Therefore, it could not develop into a standard literary language. Moreover, after the Treaty of Trianon [1920], Rusyn was heard much less than before, because the Czech rulers of Subcarpathia did their best to stamp out all memory and connections with Hungary.

After the World War I, a strong desire for education spread among the Rusyns of Subcarpathia. Returning from the western front and from prisoner-of-war camps, Rusyn soldiers realized the backwardness of those who had remained at home. Their desire was to develop literature, scholarship, and art that was appropriate for an educated society. Although they had limited resources, they did not wish to wait, and this is the reason they called on neighboring nations for help. They did not know—or did not want to recognize—that they had to talk to the common folk in its own language. They also did not realize that if the Rusyns would restore their own language through publication in newspapers, books, and journals they would gain pride and self respect.

In 1922, supporters of the unity of a common Russian language established in Uzhhorod the Dukhnovych Society, of which the first president was Evmenii Sabov who remained in that post until his death in 1934. The scholarly journal of the society was *Karpatskii krai* (Uzhhorod, 1923-24) and later *Karpatskii sviet* (Uzhhorod, 1928-38). Scholars with a real Russian education could not understand why some Subcarpathian Rusyns made such great efforts to write in Russian. This was most openly stated by Ilia Ehrenburg, a well known Russian writer who visited Subcarpathia in 1934 and who candidly expounded at length on this matter in his travelogue, *In the Jungles of Europe*:

> In Subcarpathian Rus', there are only a few educated men, yet even these are mainly occupied with debates over language. They haggle over whether their tongue is Russian, Ukrainian, or Subcarpathian Rusyn. The newspaper *Karpatorusskii golos* is published in the Russian language. But what the editors of this newspaper wish to achieve escapes my comprehension. The title of the editorial page is 'God is With Us'. Clippings from a Soviet Russian newspaper follow. Then an obscure Uzhhorod diplomat

writes in this hilarious paper: 'Moscow and the churchbells of Moscow will have a decisive influence on the European question, in the re-establishment of the modern world. Litvinov travels to the United States, to Rome, to Warsaw. Attention is paid to him! Everywhere people learn Russian. An inseparable fate ties Carpatho-Russians to Moscow. And while the world trembles before the face of Russian power, the unfortunate Carpatho-Russians must rely on a makeshift and artificial dialect. Yet in our land they light Christmas candles the same way as in Russia, they act the same way. The world expects peace from Moscow and the Soviet Union'.[62]

This mocking travel report provides a good insight into the muddled conditions in Subcarpathia and the distorted perceptions of the Russophiles during the Czech occupation. The supporters of the Ukrainian language were just as misinformed.

The followers of the Russian orientation were separated from their [Subcarpathian] land of birth and they lived in a dreamland. They learned the Russian language from books and from immigrants. They denied any relationship with the language the Rusyn people actually spoke. They did not even want to know it, because spoken Rusyn was not a "high-class" language. It was only a tongue of "commoners." During the Czech occupation, these "high-class" individuals were just like the Russophile Slovaks, Russophile Serbs, and Russophile Slovenes in the nineteenth century, some of whom tried to prove a supposed Russian origin of their own languages and to promote [Russian] linguistic unity in eastern Europe. But the majority of people in Slovak, Slovene, and Serbian inhabited territories could not understand Russian newspapers and periodicals, and only members of the intelligentsia who knew Russian had some idea of those texts.

Andrei Karabelesh (1906-1964), a poet and *gymnasium* teacher, was the pride of the Subcarpathian Russophiles. He was an unparalleled imitator. This was his sole strength. Almost every poem can be shown to be a copy of a poem by some Russian writer, whether Pushkin, Lermontov, Fet, or another. Karabelesh's poetry is anachronistic, and instead of reflecting the spirit of his own times he is concerned with the sentiment of the early nineteenth century. In that context, he published beautiful translations of "The Song of the Prisoners," a poem by the Magyar priest-poet *László Mécs* and two other Hungarian poems. The Russophile trend also included the poets Mikhail Popovych (1908-1955), Emelian Balets'kyi (1919-1986), Andrei Patrus (1917-19), and Pavel S. Fedor (1884-1952).

Among Russian-language prose writers, it is worth mentioning Nikolai Horniak-Laborchanyn, Aleksei Farynych-Makovchanyn and M. Kozyk, who wrote several dramatic works. However, one should not think that these were masterpieces; after all, not even the Russians and the Poles had written outstanding dramatic works. Here we are not talking about quality, only quantity, since before then, in the nineteenth century, Rusyn writers produced only three plays, and of those only one by Dukhnovych was generally known. Now, during the Czech occupation, plays were manufactured by the dozen. Antonii Bobul's'kyi (1877-194?) was the most industrious dramatist. He moved from Cracow to Uzhhorod, where he worked as a superintendent of a printing company. He learned both Russian and Rusyn and became a Rusyn writer. Amateur theatrical groups particularly appreciated his plays, because they are spiced with Rusyn anecdotes and word-games. But it was a work by Sion Sil'vai (1876-1932), the musical "Marusia" with a score by the author as well, that gained the greatest popularity. It is a pleasant though somewhat naive piece that was often performed by Subcarpathian Rusyns as well as by their immigrant brethren in America.

Writers belonging to the Ukrainian orientation lived as well in a fantasy land. They objected to the language spoken in Subcarpathia by the common Rusyn people, because in their view it was a primitive tongue in comparison with the more developed Ukrainian language. The Ukrainophiles grouped around the Prosvita cultural society founded in 1920. Their scholarly journal, *Naukovyi zbôrnyk* (Uzhhorod, 1922-38), mainly published studies by immigrants from the Ukraine.

Among the better Subcarpathian poets were Vasyl' Grendzha-Dons'kyi (1897-1974), Iulii Borshosh-Kumiats'kyi (1905-1978), Zoreslav (Sevastiian Sabol, b. 1909), and Stefanova Bozhuk (1907-1939). The most versatile and closest to the Rusyn orientation was Borshosh-Kumiats'kyi, who was influenced by modern Hungarian poets. He wrote fine poetry that dealt with social problems.

Among the prose writers worth mentioning were Luka Demian (1894-1968), Aleksander Markush (1891-1971), and Iryna Nevyts'ka (1886-1965). The picturesque descriptions of nature and the humorous stories Markush took from the life of the common folk are exquisite. He learned from such Hungarian writers as Tömörkény, Mikszáth, and Móra[pp] to observe carefully peasants and their sentiments. Moreover, the language of Markush is closer to Rusyn than to Ukrainian and his outlook is clearly Rusyn. The Ukrainian group had no dramatist.

Literary life was certainly alive during the Czech occupation, but the writers (with few exemptions) wrote either in Russian or Ukrainian. Almost no one enriched Rusyn literature. The Czechs did not favor this, even though both the Dukhnovych Society and Prosvita Society received grants and other forms of support for that purpose. Instead, the Czechs aided both literary trends in order to divide the Rusyns and eradicate all attempts for the development of a united Rusyn national spirit. In the end, they did succeed in creating friction between Subcarpathia's Russophiles and Ukrainophiles, which led to antagonism that sometimes grew to a hatred so great that they did not even read each other's writings. As a result, neither influenced the other.

pp. István Tömörkény (1866-1917), Kálmán Mikszáth (1847-1910), and Ferenc Móra (1879-1934) were writers who belonged to the realist school of Hungarian literature, best known for their short stories and tales dealing with the life of the peasantry and poor classes.

CHAPTER SEVEN

Rusyn Folk Poetry

Folk poetry is as old as the people itself. It is born as soon as the language of a smaller or larger group of people develops. It progresses together with the evolution of a given society, reflecting the experience and the culture of the people. The peculiarity of this phenomemon is that it embraces the entire folk. Its main merit is the truth. As [the philosopher, literary critic, and ethnographer] János Erdélyi (1814-1868) said: "What we find in it [folk poetry] are true facts. If it refers to history, it is history. If it refers to morals, it is morality. If it refers to taste, it is the taste. Here all syllables are data, and all data of the past is the root of the future. . ."[63] It is unfortunate that the Rusyns preserved very little data from the past. Nobody bothered to write down the relics of their folk poetry.

Rusyn folk songs, which are the prototype of folk poetry, could tell a lot about the people, because they flourished freely among the hills and valleys of Subcarpathia. If during the Middle Ages Hungarian secular songs, the so-called "flower songs" mainly dealing with love, were persecuted by the church, no one persecuted the songs of the Rusyns. Moreover, until the middle of the nineteenth century, the Rusyns did not have a so-called educated class which would have felt embarrassed by the vulgar contents of such songs. The medieval Rusyn priest had no more education than the Rusyn peasant farmer. He worked beside him in the fields and he sang the same songs. Nor was the Rusyn folksong regarded as something bad in the nineteenth century, because the educated class consisted almost exclusively of priests. This segment of society simply did not pay any attention one way or the other to folksongs or folk poetry.

"Rusyn folk-poetry. Too bad so far no one has dealt with it seriously. There is a large number of folksongs living on the lips of the rural people."[64] So wrote a Rusyn priest in the official weekly of the

Greek Catholic clergy and school teachers, the *Görög katolikus sze-mle*. Apparently, the author of that article was not familiar with Teodor Lehoczky's book printed three decades earlier, *Magyarországi orosz népdalok* (Hungary's Rusyn Folksongs, 1864), Mihály Fincicki's *Magyar-orosz népdalok* (Uhro-Rusyn Folksongs, 1870), nor the publications of Russian and Ukrainian scholars.[65]

The Rusyns are a musical folk. They sing about all events in their lives, whether happy or sad. With originality and force the unspoiled Rusyn spirit is expressed in these songs. Rusyns sing whether working at home or under the free skies of the Lord. Most are love songs. Many originate from life in the military and many depict the everyday life of man, personal emotion, or longing for the homeland when far away with the armed forces or work crews. Some deal with an actual event or situation. It is interesting to note that while the majority of the Rusyns always lived near the forest, they never created hunting songs. The mountain creeks, rivers, and lakes of the Rusyn hills abound with fish, but there are no fishing songs. Why is this so? Because neither hunting nor fishing ever formed the livelihood of Rusyns. And apart from the eastern side of the Verkhovyna, there are no songs about outlaws.

The Rusyn folksong is similar to the Hungarian. An illustration from nature is used to underline a mood, and often parallels are drawn between nature and the life of man:

> On every tree limbs grow,
> Birds sit in pairs in a row,
> Only I wait in vain
> For a mate, who never came.

To express a specific mood, the folksong uses scenes taken from nature. A large number of these became symbolic, and these symbols remain unchanged for centuries. For example, a coniferous tree is the symbol of sadness; the oak represents manliness; the birch or ash is the symbol for girls and generally for females; the owl suggests a sad woman; the falcon symbolizes a young man. In Rusyn folksongs, a girl is often called "small fish":

> My sweet little dove, my tiny golden fish

It is not difficult to understand that in Rusyn folksongs only plants and animals common to Subcarpathia are mentioned. If someone were to list the animals, birds, insects, and plants mentioned in Rusyn folksongs, the result would be a veritable inventory of the animal and plant world of the Carpathians. On the other hand, the geography depicted in the songs is not precise. The Danube River and the sea are often mentioned. Information about the Danube comes from the fact that the Tysa flows through the Danubian Basin, while it is through fables that Rusyns heard about the sea—which is thousands of miles away.

Other information from folksongs deals with occupations. Peasants and shepherds are most frequently mentioned, whereas merchants and tradesmen always appear as foreigners. This is because merchants and tradesmen are very seldom found among Rusyns. If a member of the intelligentsia is mentioned, it is a priest, cantor, magistrate, or town clerk. Why? Because these members of the intelligentsia are mostly Rusyns.

Three-fourths of all Rusyn folksongs deal with love. The topic is the same as in love songs of other nations. A peculiarity of the Rusyn folksong is that some deal with a mother's advice regarding marriage. The religious Rusyn does not appreciate the marriage of a son to a widow or of a girl to a widower. This is expressed in this song:

> Marry, my dear son, and let a girl be your spouse,
> The heart of a girl is like sunshine in summer;
> While at times it shines sadly, it brings warmth into
> the house.

> Marry, my dear son, but don't bring home a widow;
> Because the widow's heart is like sunshine in winter,
> While it warms, the wind blasts colder.

Next to love songs, those referring to the armed forces are the most frequent. The enlisted man is sad; he has to leave his parents, his lover, his village. Yet if he already wears a uniform, he is proud of it. He brags about his desire to fight the French or the Turks. It is interesting that only these two nations are ever mentioned as enemies.

> Greetings to you emperor, my good emperor, my royal emperor!
> We defeated the French, and I long to go home.
> Greetings to you emperor, my good emperor, you made me a
> soldier;
> Do me the favor to enlist also my lover!
> Help us, good Lord, to beat the Turks,
> And in that nice country to embrace the girls.

In love songs, only Subcarpathian villages are mentioned. In soldier songs, Hungarian and Austrian towns where the enlisted had to report or where they were stationed are listed. Rusyns served mainly at Sighet (Máramorossziget), Mukachevo, Uzhhorod, Levoča (Lőcse), Košice, and Vienna.

> Don't cry my rose, don't cry
> Because you'll cry out your eyes.
> Levoča is a faraway place
> Where they take me in haste.

> A bloody creek flows
> Near Uzhhorod with a splash,
> My loving rose inquires if my skull was crushed?
> No, it is not blood of that sort.

> It is not from my head,
> It is my enemy's instead,
> Cut in pieces by my sword.

The one or two Rusyn soldier songs that deal with the Cossacks originate from Galicia, and they appeared only during the Czech occupation in Subcarpathia.

A significant feature of folksongs is that they migrate from place to place and change when they enter another nation's poetry. Rusyn raftsmen who were in Szolnok and Szeged, located along the Tysa/Tisza River in the Hungarian plain, learned many Hungarian folksongs and sang them either in Hungarian or in a literal Rusyn translation. Such titles as "Szeretnék szántani, hat ökrőt hajtani" (I would like to plow and drive six oxen); "Káka tövén költ a ruca" (The loon lays her eggs at the bottom of the bullrush); "Azt mondják nem adnak engem galambomnak" (They say I may not marry, my dove); "Ha bemegyek a templomba" (When I go to the church); "Debrecenbe kéne menni, pulykakakast kéne venni" (We must go to Debrecen, we have to buy a turkey-rooster) are generally well known in Subcarpathia.

Ballads are the real pearls of Rusyn folk poetry. The people especially like them and usually do not stop singing them until the end. They are liked not so much for their musical sound as for their content. One of the more well-known ballads tells a tale about a young man who was refused permission to marry his sweetheart.

I leave, yes I go
Across the hill, through the valley,
Never more will I see her,
If she was not meant for me anyway.

If you were not meant for me
Oh, my girl, good-bye;
Good-bye, my dear girl,
For you faithful heart I loved you.

Through four long years
Your faithful heart I loved,
Yet for four Sundays
I didn't see my beloved.
I didn't see my beloved
On those four Sundays
And next day our hearts pained
From our farewell.

The poor lad suffered
From fever in the green forest,
The dying girl was protected
By the parental nest.

For the dear girl
Bells are ringing,
For the poor boy
The wolves are howling.

For the girl
Sad parents are crying,
For the poor lad only
The crows are crowing.

The most popular form of Rusyn folk song is the *kolomiika*.

I go to the mountain range
Where the Boikos dwelled,
Where they hack up the music
While dancing they yelled.

The first line has eight and the second six syllables. The main feature in the Rusyn original is that the accent is to fall on the syllable before the last and that the second line should rhyme with the fourth. Nonetheless, most *kolomiiky* deviate from this norm and have four lines, each having six syllables:

> How nice for me, dear mother,
> To live along the Tysa,
> There I see my lover
> Bring his horse to water.

> In the deep green forest
> The songs of birds are ringing,
> It's good to make a lovenest,
> Where nobody is looking.

Most remarkable are Rusyn songs depicting historical events. It is particularly unfortunate that there are fewer songs about historical events and that the old ones have been forgotten. The present generation is interested in new songs and only of current times. For instance, the struggle for freedom led by Rákóczi and the destruction of the Labanz placed many fine songs in the hearts of Rusyns.

> The Magyars are oppressed,
> The Germans are uplifted,
> Our freedoms are vanishing
> And nothing left is sacred.

> Our precious freedoms
> Were taken away with a strong hand
> By those awful Germans
> Who tore asunder the fatherland.

> They tore apart Poland,
> They are tearing apart Hungary
> They regard these lands
> As just another wilderness.

Unfortunately, the present generation no longer remembers those beautiful folksongs from feudal times when the Rusyn serf transformed his sad life into verses and song.

Folk prose, whether legends, tales, proverbs, or aphorisms, are abundant among the Rusyns. These texts are versatile and reflect the people's religious beliefs, morals, level of knowledge, and imagination. They were drawn mostly from the *sbornyky* that were fashionable in the seventeenth and eighteenth centuries.

The Rusyns love proverbs and frequently spice their conversation with them. Proverbs reflect poignant observance of life situations: "Dismount a strange horse, even if you are in the middle of puddle"; "God is high above, the king far away"; "Heavy is the loaded back pack, the empty one is even heavier"; "The wife supports three walls of the household, the husband only one"; "For the poor man it is difficult even to run down the hill, the rich man is able to go up running"; "A man who has eaten enough does not believe the hungry man"; "Don't laugh at a funeral, don't cry at a wedding"; "When an old woman descends from a carriage, the wheel spokes have it easier."

In Rusyn folklore, we fail to find (with the exception of some recently acquired Cossack songs) any Ukrainian or Polish traditions or memories. Rusyn folk literature reveals nothing of Cossack revolts nor of the bloody wars in Poland and the Ukraine. The most typical product of Ukrainian folk poetry, the *duma* or epic poem, is unknown in Subcarpathia. While the heroes of Ukrainian folk poetry are Khmel'nyts'kyi, Mazepa, and Doroshenko, the heroes of Rusyns are King Mátyás, Rákóczi, and Kossuth.[qq] It was only during the Czech occupation that Rusyns heard for the first time about the Sich, that olden Cossack camp in Zaporozhia, which is the pride of Galician and southern Rus' folksongs.

The Subcarpathian Rusyns have an ideology which is different from that of the Galician Ukrainians. The settlers who moved to the southern slopes of the Carpathian Mountains soon became divorced from the attitudes and feelings of their ethnically related brethren [to the north] and instead assimilated with the Magyars and adjusted to Hungary. This was already seen by the author of the eighteenth-century Latin chronical originating from the village of Huklyvyi (Zúgó): "While it is only a hundred years ago that the first Rusyn settlers came to the Verkhovyna, the Carpathian Mountains not only separate Hungary from Poland, they also separate the people from their [former] customs and morals."[66]

---

qq. Bohdan Khmel'nyts'kyi (ca. 1595-1657), Petro Doroshenko (1627-1698), and Ivan Mazepa (1639-1709) were among the most outstanding leaders (hetmans) of the Zaporozhian Cossacks who beginning in 1648 tried to carve out an autonomous political entity in the Ukraine through conflict with Poland and Muscovy.

The reference to the heroes of Hungarian history are to Mátyás Corvinus (reigned 1458-1490), the renaissance king, and to the seventeenth-century Prince Ferenc Rákóczi II and Lajos Kossuth (see above pp. 22-25).

CHAPTER EIGHT

Religion and the Church

The Greek Catholic Church

In the thirteenth and fourteenth centuries the Rusyns of Subcarpathia had no organized church. No priest followed the first settlers to Subcarpathia and, therefore, no allotments for clergy were put aside by landlords when the villages were built. Subsequently, when the settlers built a church and received a priest, they had to come up with means for his upkeep.

The first step toward an organized church began with the founding of the Basilian monastery of Mukachevo. The ecclesiastical head of the Orthodox population in Subcarpathia and neighboring counties was the archimandrite (hegumen) of the Mukachevo monastery. The first archimandrite was presbyter Lukach, who held the authority of bishop between 1439 and 1445. It is from those years that the origin of the Mukachevo Eparchy can be dated. This is further substantiated by a report of Cardinal Lippay sent to Rome in 1651:

> It was told to me by Partenii, bishop of Mukachevo, that he saw royal documents about 150 years old regarding the establishment of the monastery and the Eparchy of Mukachevo. . . . In my opinion, however, this foundation refers [only] to the monastery. The foundation of the eparchy happened when, with the consent of the patriarch of Constantinople, the [Orthodox] bishops who became alienated [from the Greek Catholic Church] founded at the monastery of Mukachevo a schismatic eparchy.[67]

According to canon law and the laws of Hungary, the Orthodox Eparchy of Mukachevo existed in name only. It was not canonized. Not even the landlords of the Mukachevo-Chynadiievo estate regarded the archimandrite of the Mukachevo monastery as bishop.

They treated him as they wished, without any respect. As for the Orthodox village priests, they had the legal status of serfs and were poor, uneducated, and ignorant. Not even the archimandrite of the [Mukachevo] monastery excelled in theological training.

Count György Drugeth, lord of the estates at Humenné and Uzhhorod, decided to improve the poor status of the Rusyn clergy. He knew that the Orthodox Rusyns who lived in Poland in 1595 had united with Rome,[rr] and soon after the Roman Catholic church trained and educated Greek Catholic priests. They also received the same privileges enjoyed by Roman Catholic priests.

After extensive negotiations, the clergy of Szepes, Sáros, and Ung counties accepted the church union in 1646. With this act, the path to western civilization was opened to the Rusyns of Hungary. The ruling princes of Transylvania, however, objected to the union with Rome. Therefore, the clergy and the population of the counties of Bereg and Máramaros became Greek Catholic only much later, when this territory finally broke away from Protestant Transylvania. Consequently, until 1735, the Rusyns had both a Greek Catholic and an Orthodox bishop.

The decision of the clergy to unify with Rome was motivated by the privileges they gained as well as by a desire for unified religious beliefs. It was to be some time, however, before the Greek Catholic clergy received the anticipated advantages. Large land allotments were given to Greek Catholic parishes (for the use of priests and cantors), while the clergy received the same privileges and was governed by the same canon law and local customs allowed the Roman Catholic clergy. After the 1646 church union, the Greek Catholic clergy was placed under the jurisdiction of the [Roman Catholic] archbishop of Eger, [and the new religious authorities] immediately realized the need to educate dependable priests, since this task was not adequately taken care of by the Orthodox monastery of Mukachevo.

In time, when the first educated Greek Catholic priests graduated from universities and Roman Catholic seminaries, they felt the "foster-parent" attitude of Eger archdiocese to be degrading. The result was a movement to obtain an independent eparchy and

---

rr. The process of church union begun in Rome in 1595 and concluded at Brest in Poland (now Brest-Litovsk in the Belorussian S.S.R.) in 1596 affected all Orthodox believers in the eastern regions of the Polish-Lithuanian Commonwealth. These included primarily ethnic Ukrainians and Belorussians, together referred to at the time in official documents as Ruthenians.

seminary for Mukachevo, a movement that ended with a victory for the Greek Catholic clergy.

In 1771, at the request of Maria Theresa, Empress of Austria and Queen of Hungary, Pope Clement XIV canonized the Mukachevo Greek Catholic Eparchy. At the time, the territory of the eparchy extended to 13 counties and included 711 parishes. Later, its extent was substantially reduced. First, in 1777, several parishes of the Mukachevo eparchy were attached to the then newly-established Oradea (Nagyvárad) Romanian Greek Catholic Eparchy. Then, in 1816, the Prešov Eparchy was detached from Mukachevo. Later, on June 8, 1912, Pope Pius X established with the bull *Christi fideles graeci* the Hajdúdorog Greek Catholic Eparchy, to which 60 villages were detached from the Mukachevo Eparchy. Finally, the dictated Treaty of Trianon gave about 20,000 Greek Catholic Rusyns to Romania in 1920. Thus, on the eve of the Czech occupation of Subcarpathia (1920), the Eparchy of Mukachevo had 320 parishes.

Administratively, the Mukachevo Eparchy is divided into five vicariates: Berehovo, Máramaros, Ugocsa, Ung, and Zemplén, which, in turn, are subdivided into 39 deaneries. The first bishop of the canonized eparchy[ss] was Andrei Bachyns'kyi (1732-1809, consecrated 1793), who transferred the eparchial seat from Mukachevo to Uzhhorod.

Because the Rusyns were a poor people, they could not provide funds to build a cathedral, a bishop's residence, dwelling places for canons, a seminary building, or other edifices. Therefore, Empress Maria Theresa donated to the eparchy the former Jesuit church and collegium of Uzhhorod together with the Drugeth castle and all buildings belonging to it. The [Austrian] treasury provided funds to make the buildings suitable for ecclesiastical purposes. Eight canonic seats were established in the eparchial see.

The first bishop of the Mukachevo Eparchy, Andrei Bachyns'kyi, did much to support the education and upkeep of the Rusyn clergy and the members of the teaching profession. It was because of his intervention that Empress Maria Theresa founded a seminary for theologians, while the bishop himself undertook the construction of a college for cantor-teachers. Bachyns'kyi also collected all the old books and documents which were dispersed throughout individual

---

ss. Actually, Ivan Bradach (1732-1772), who had held the title of "apostolic vicar" to the Eparchy of Mukachevo, remained at his post after being consecrated bishop in 1771.

parishes, and with them he laid the foundation for an episcopal library and archive.

Bishop Aleksei Povchii (1753-1831, consecrated 1816) erected the Orphanotrophium, a house for orphaned sons of priests who attended *gymnasium*, while during the reign of Bishop Ivan Pastelii (1826-1891, consecrated 1875), the Alumneum college was built for non-orphaned sons of priests who attended *gymnasium*. Pastelii also erected a student dormitory. The reigning bishops of Mukachevo during the Czech occupation were Antonii Papp (1867-1945, consecrated 1912), Petro Gebei (1864-1931, consecrated 1924), and Aleksander Stoika (1890-1943, consecrated 1932).

In 1919, the Eparchy of Mukachevo had 384 public schools, but during the Czech occupation almost all were closed, because the government did not pay for them and local parishes had insufficient funds. The Czech government even persecuted such schools, considering religious and moral education unimportant. Moreover, the government worried, in particular, that the Greek Catholic public schools would foster ties with Hungary.

Five monasteries are located within the territory of the Mukachevo Eparchy: Uzhhorod, Mukachevo, Imstycheve (Miszticze), Malyi Bereznyi (Kisberezná), and Boroniava (Husztbaranya).

The Eparchy of Prešov (Eperjes) was founded in 1818 by Pope Pius VII. It has eight canons who assist the bishop. The former church of the Minorite order in Prešov, built in 1673, was rebuilt as a Greek Catholic cathedral. The first bishop of the new eparchy was Hryhorii Tarkovych (1754-1841, consecrated 1821), who spent almost all his time with his books, so that actually the affairs of the eparchy were taken care of by his secretary, Vasyl' Popovych (1796-1864), who himself later [1837] became bishop of Mukachevo. The second bishop at Prešov was a Slavophile, Iosyf Gaganets' (1793-1875, consecrated 1843), and it was because of his intervention that the [Hungarian] government permitted the establishment of the Saint Basil Society in 1867.

Much was done for the organization of the Prešov Eparchy under Bishop Ivan Valyi (1837-1911, consecrated 1882). Before Valyi's reign, his priests and cantor-teachers had to be educated at Uzhhorod, so he built a seminary and a teacher's college in Prešov. This was only one of many things he did to raise the cultural level of the priests and the people. The Prešov Eparchy had four vicariates—[based in the historic counties of] Abaúj-Torna, Gömör, Szepes, and

Zemplén—and 19 deaconries. The Eparchy of Prešov also had Greek Catholic parishes in Bratislava (Pozsony) and Prague.

The Orthodox Church

All Rusyns were originally Orthodox until 1646, when a split occurred from both the religious and organizational standpoint. Those Rusyns who lived in Bereg and Máramaros counties and who were administratively attached to Transylvania, remained Orthodox; the rest united with Rome. In 1664, the Orthodox bishop was evicted from the monastery of Mukachevo and Petro Partenii, a Greek Catholic, took his place. Not long after this, the entire population of Bereg county which had been Orthodox became Greek Catholic. Only Máramaros county remained Orthodox. Finally, in 1734, when the last Orthodox bishop of Máramaros, Dositei, died in the monastery at Ubl'a (Ublya), all Orthodox believers of Máramaros joined the union with Rome. In 1769, as a result of agitation in some villages of Máramaros, some people wanted to return to Orthodoxy, but before long the movement calmed down.

Throughout the nineteenth century, Rusyns remained loyal to the Greek Catholic faith. At the end of the century, however, because of the bad economic situation in Subcarpathia, many Rusyns emigrated to the United States where they fell under the influence of Russian propagandists. Russian-American priests persuaded many Rusyns to convert to the Orthodox faith. Particularly effective in this regard was deacon Aleksei Toth (1853-1909), who was of Rusyn origin.[tt] Toth quarrelled with his Catholic bishop, became a Russian citizen, and [in 1891] entered the service of the Russian bishop of San Francisco. He also published a well-written booklet entitled, *Gde iskati pravda?* (Where Should We Seek the Truth, 1894), which was eagerly read by Rusyns who lived in the United States and who smuggled a few copies into Hungary.

Toth knew how the Rusyns thought and he could speak their language. That every line was in complete contrast to the truth was not evident to the naive reader. For instance, Toth wrote that the Greek Catholic religion was invented in Poland by two godless Polish bishops to persecute the Orthodox Rusyns. Their devilish plan was successful. The new Greek Catholic priests were even more vicious than the Roman Catholics. They destroyed the graves of the Orthodox

---

tt. Before coming to America in 1889, Toth was a professor at the seminary and chancellor of the Greek Catholic Eparchy of Prešov.

dead, whose coffins were exhumed. They beat and murdered the Orthodox priests and leased their churches to the Jews. But God had enough of the Orthodox suffering and punished the Poles. By God's will, the emperors of Austria and Prussia and the fatherly tsar (*batiushka*) [of Russia] divided Poland among themselves in order to stop the Poles from persecuting further God's dear Orthodox children. As for Hungary, Toth continued, the union with Rome happened in a similar fashion. Extremist [Roman Catholic] Hungarian bishops persecuted Orthodox true believers in the same manner as happened in Poland. They lured the Orthodox priests with promises, and in this way persuaded 70 of the 1000 to accept the Union of Uzhhorod [1646]. The others were thrown into jail, where they were tortured and threatened with exile unless they denied their true [Orthodox] faith.

The real truth is that the first Greek Catholic bishop, Vasylii Tarasovych (1633-1651) was persecuted for his union with Rome by the ruling prince of Transylvania, György Rákóczi (1591-1648), who at the time owned the Mukachevo-Chynadiievo estate. Bishop Tarasovych was kept prisoner in the dungeon of Rákóczi's castle and later was driven out of the land. Many Greek Catholic priests suffered a similar fate in Subcarpathia.

The religious agitation from [Rusyn immigrants in] the United States was parallelled by agitation coming from Russia. Because of propaganda by Rusyns who returned to Subcarpathia from the United States, in 1902 one-third of the Greek Catholic population of Becherov (Biharó) in the Sáros county returned to Orthodoxy. Becherov was followed in 1903 by Iza (Máramaros county) and Velyki Luchky (Bereg county). When it found out about this religious propaganda, aided as it was with tsarist Russian money and moral support, the Hungarian government brought the Orthodox leaders to court. Each served 14 months in jail. Nonetheless, after their release they continued their proselytization, and through the Gerovskii brothers[uu] in Chernivtsi [in neighboring Austrian Bukovina] they received help and money from Russia. When the government collected enough evidence regarding the political nature of the [Orthodox] religious movement, the state prosecutor brought charges against 94 agitators at the royal court of Sighet (Máramarossziget). The charges put forth

---

uu. Aleksei Gerovskii (1883-1972) and Georgii Gerovskii (1886-1959) were grandsons of the leading nineteenth-century Subcarpathian Rusyn Russophile activist, Adol'f Dobrians'kyi.

on July 13, 1913 were: instigating rebellion against the Hungarian state, the Greek Catholic religion, and the Catholic clergy. On March 3, 1914, after the charges were proved to be true, 32 of the accused were convicted. The high court and the supreme court of Hungary confirmed the jail sentences.

After [World War I] and the occupation of Subcarpathia, the Czech government strove to convert as many Rusyns as possible to Orthodoxy, hoping in this way to weaken the magyarone or pro-Hungarian orientation of the Greek Catholic Church. Orthodox priests would claim that "the dominant attitude of the Greek Catholics is magyarone, even if they do not admit it openly." The Czech government held the same view. Thus, during the first years of the Czech occupation, Greek Catholic priests were relentlessly persecuted and suppressed. At the same time, the Orthodox faith, the Russian Orthodox Church, and its clergy were supported. Many of the Czech Legionnaires[vv] returning from Russia even brought Russian Orthodox wives with them, and when the Legionnaires were given military posts in Subcarpathian Rus', they gave support to the uneducated Orthodox priests and other local agents of Orthodoxy as well as Russian Orthodox émigrés. Backed by the Legionnaires and the Czech state administration, persecution of the Greek Catholic clergy continued. In many villages, the local Greek Catholic priest was evicted from his home as the Czech police looked on and an Orthodox priest, with no qualifications whatsoever, replaced him. The alienated and persecuted Greek Catholic Church fought heroically against Czech-supported Orthodoxy, and when the struggle finally ended, between 22 and 24 percent of Rusyn Greek Catholics had converted to Orthodoxy.

In Subcarpathian Rus', Orthodox churches were built with Czechoslovak government support. The government also appointed the priests. By 1938, about half of the Orthodox clergy received annual monetary assistance (*congrua*) from the Czechoslovak government. The Orthodox priests themselves admitted that they would not

---

vv. The Legionnaires were part of a Czechoslovak Army established in Russia during the summer of 1917 from former Czech prisoners-of-war who had their own unit in the Russian imperial army. Unable to reach the European front directly, they moved eastward across Siberia (fighting Bolshevik units during the Russian Civil War along the way). When they finally reached western Europe (after World War I was over) and returned to their homeland (now the new state of Czechoslovakia) in late 1918, they were hailed as heroes.

have survived had it not been for official support, because Orthodox propaganda had no success among the more wealthy and educated Rusyns.

Orthodox priests were taught to perform colorful services and they learned some church history. Those who studied in Belgrade had some courses in dogma as well. With regard to the Orthodox past in the Subcarpathian lands, they had to know the following:

> The acceptance of Orthodoxy in Subcarpathian Rus' occurred before the Christianization of Kievan Rus', that is before 988 AD. At that time, the Bulgarian Slavs were the neighbors of the Subcarpathian Rusyns, who lived on the plain between the rivers Danube and Tysa. They adapted religion from the Bulgars, which was spread by the pupils of the famed apostles of the Slavs, Cyril and Methodius. The first priests in Subcarpathia were Bulgars. Only after Kiev had been converted to Christianity did priests begin to come to Subcarpathia in order to strengthen the faith of the population and to build monasteries. Orthodoxy, or as the people call it, the old faith [*stara vira*], penetrated thoroughly the life of the people. This is the reason that it was able to survive the tempestuous year of the Magyar invasion (896 AD) and to remain unharmed after the Turkish conquest of Hungary (1526). Orthodoxy also survived the years of internal strife that followed, when churches, monasteries, and villages were laid to ruin. . . .[68]

These and similar "historical truths" were taught to Orthodox seminarians by their leading scholars, the monk Aleksei Dekhterev and Georgii Gerovskii.

Since there was no one among the [local] Orthodox priests who would have been able to organize the church, the Serbian Orthodox Church sent (in 1921) Dositei, the bishop of Niš, who organized and led the church until 1926. Irinei, the Serbian Orthodox bishop of Novi Sad (Újvidék) followed him in 1927. His [Serbian Orthodox] successors were in 1928-1929 Serafim, bishop of Prizren, and finally from 1930 to 1931, Iosif, bishop of Bitola. It was due to the efforts of Iosif that on July 20, 1931, the Orthodox eparchy of Mukachevo was established. Then on October 2, 1931, a conference of Serbian bishops elected their fellow Serbian bishop, Damaskin, to be the bishop of the Orthodox Rusyns with the title: Bishop of Mukachevo and Prešov. Damaskin returned to Yugoslavia in 1938 at which time the Serbian bishop's conference appointed Vladimir Raich to the Mukachevo see.

The Mukachevo-Prešov Orthodox eparchy has five large monasteries, three for men and two for women. Those for men are the St. Nicholas Monastery near Iza, the Transfiguration Monastery near Tereblia (Talaborfalu, Máramaros county), and St. Iov Monastery near Ladomirová (Ladomérvágás, Sáros county). The women's monasteries are in Lipsha (Lipcse, Máramaros county) and Dombok (Domboká, Bereg county). St. Iov's Monastery has a printing shop, which issues sacred books, missals, almanacs, and newspapers. Beside these establishments, there are also five smaller male monasteries.

The aim of the Serbian bishops was to secure learned priests for the Orthodox Rusyns. Into their small seminary were sent those who had a basic education, the equivalent of today's grade eight. In 1936, there were even two high school graduates who were sent to the Orthodox theological faculty in Belgrade. According to 1936 statistics, the Mukachevo-Prešov Orthodox eparchy had 127 churches, 138 ordained priests, and 140,000 faithful.

CHAPTER NINE

Economic Conditions

For the first two or three centuries following their immigration to Hungary, the Rusyns lived in prosperity. Their material situation was better than that of the Magyar serfs. Therefore, it is incorrect to assert, as the writings of Russian and Ukrainian historians suggest, that Rusyn serfs lived like the Magyar serfs. This view is based on the study by the Magyar historian Ignác Acsádi,[69] whose description of Magyar serfs was applied by Ukrainian and Russian writers to the Rusyns, but without any research or proof.

Two laws, No. III of 1481 and No. XLV of 1495, freed the Rusyns from paying taxes to the king. This was a great concession in comparison with the burden of the Magyar serfs. However, the royal court disliked the freedom from taxation of the Rusyns, and our kings and later the emperors in Vienna beginning in the sixteenth century demanded that the parliament withdraw the above-mentioned laws. In 1569, the court at Vienna commissioned three officials, Salm, Pappendorf, and Paczot to travel through the Rusyn-inhabited areas of Hungary. They reported that all Rusyns lived well and would be able to pay the tithe and other taxes to the king and emperor.

Based on this report, in 1572, Emperor Maximilian II (reigned 1564-1576) demanded from the diet (parliament) and from the Assembly of the Nobles that they declare the Rusyns equal to the Magyars with respect to tax burdens. "It is incredible that the Magyars, the masters of the country, should pay the *dica*[ww] and tithe, while the Rusyns . . . who are newcomers and strangers . . . remain freemen and be exempt from taxes as if they were to be nobler and better than the Magyars."[70] The reply of the nobles was that the ex-

---

ww. The *dica* was a unit for assessment of the tax-paying capacity of individual serf families.

emption from the tithe should be maintained because it was a right secured in an earlier decree issued by King Mátyás Corvinus (reigned 1458-1490) and later reaffirmed by Ulászló II (reigned 1490-1516).

Later, the Szepes county royal council reported as follows: ". . . they [the Rusyns] almost never sow; they prefer animal husbandry and devastate the best forests, turning them into grazing areas and often reducing good agricultural soil into pastures. They conduct large scale cattle trade and have several good ways to make money. They are rich; they have much gold."[71] The Rusyns gave plenty to their landlords, whose new-found wealth prompted the Szepes council to declare in 1571 that the Hungarian landlord "who has a Rusyn, has a good kitchen." The Szepes county reports also indicated that the Rusyns had more privileges than they deserved. The state had given them seven to twelve years of exemption from taxes, and this privilege was often abused. After the exempt periods ran out, the settlers packed up and began a new settlement elsewhere. Thus, they were free from taxes all the time.

Their migrations, however, could not last forever. Virgin forest areas waiting to be cut down decreased, while at the same time the size of the population increased through immigration and natural growth. The landlords began to be more careful as well. They would not let Rusyns leave, and before long they had to settle down for good. If during the sixteenth century all reports speak of prosperous Rusyns with much money, by the seventeenth century poverty became synonomous with the name Rusyn.

As more and more pastures were converted into agricultural land, the Rusyns became settled farmers and poorer. Migratory herding of animals became restricted to higher elevations, and finally even ceased there. In the end, flocks and herds could be grazed only in certain alpine areas.

Rusyn prosperity was also undermined by wars, invasions, general unrest, and forced appropriations. The final reduction of the Rusyns to the status of beggars followed the defeat of the Rákóczi freedom revolution in 1711, when they were accused of having fought on the side of the *kuruc* rebels. Documents reveal several examples of destruction throughout Rusyn-inhabited areas leading up to 1711.

In 1657, about 40,000 Polish soldiers under Lubomirski stormed into Subcarpathia. As Rusyn chronicles and marginal notes in church books indicate, these troops destroyed and pillaged at will. They ransacked and burned Visk, Mukachevo and Berehovo. Marching from Szatmár county they passed through the mountains into Máramaros county driving cattle and horses ahead of them, and with tremendous booty they passed through the valley of the Tereblia on their return to Poland. Marginal notes in Rusyn church books reveal that three times during the seventeenth century Polish troops broke into Subcarpathia to loot the area.

The Kuruc-Labanc struggle also caused much suffering for Rusyns. According to the 1688 record book (*urbarium*) of the Mukachevo estate, ten villages were devastated by Polish troops. Then, in 1691, the head of the Mukachevo castle garrison reported that 40 villages were burned by foreign soldiers. An insight into the kind of damage that was done comes from a complaint of the little village of Husák (Huszák) in Ung county. Three companies of soldiers spent four days in that village, during which they took two bushels of wheat, 190 bushels of rye, 203 bushels of barley, 243 bushels of oats, and 40 carriage loads of hay, mostly from poor people. They ate 226 geese, 1 pig, 15 piglets, 3.46 florins worth of lard, 84.5 florins worth of other food, and drank 22 florins worth of wine. Besides this, the soldiers destroyed much furniture, using it at times for fuel; and by threatening to burn houses, they extorted money even from the poorest inhabitants.[71]

Similarly, a marginal note on a manuscript copy of an *Evangelium* found in the Basilian monastery in Mukachevo reads: "In the year 1703, Lord Ferenc Rákóczi came to the city of Mukachevo from Poland and stayed for three days. Soon after he left, one day early in the morning, General Montecuccoli[xx] marched in with his regiment, drove away all the people, killed many—among them innocent peasants too—and at the suggestion of the devil destroyed the city church of Orosvyhiv (Oroszvég), burned the town, and tore pages out from this book."[73]

Along with losses related directly to military activity, both men and animals were decimated by another enemy—contagious diseases. During the Rákóczi rebellion, the number of Rusyn serfs who owned property was reduced by two-thirds. Thus, if in 1704 in each village we find about twelve landowning serfs, by 1711 this number dropped to four. After the disarmament of Rákóczi's troops, the Rusyns became particularly poor. Even formerly well-to-do Rusyn peasants became

---

xx. General Raymond Montecuccoli, a count of Italian descent, was commander-in-chief of the Austrian imperial army in the late seventeenth and early eighteenth century when he often fought against Ottoman and Transylvanian armies in northeastern Hungary.

destitute. [Pro-Austrian] *labanc* soldiers drove away their cattle or ate them and new landlords confiscated their land.

The following are only a few examples of the enormous changes in the economic condition of the Rusyns. In 1645, the number of hogs in Rusyn villages was 12,885; by 1711 only 417. In 1645, the sheep stock was at 10,409; while in 1711, it was only 809. Horse and cattle stocks were reduced in the same proportions. In the first place, the prosperous land-owning Rusyn peasants were ruined because they had joined Rákóczi's army. After the defeat of the rebellion, the impoverished Rusyn could not improve his status, because the only means to prosperity—the land—was taken away from him. He did not send his sons to learn a trade or become a merchant, because the only means of living the Rusyn knew was to till the soil or raise animals.

Rákóczi's Mukachevo and Chynadiievo estates were first leased by the Austrian emperor to Baron Haber. Then, in 1721, Emperor Karl VI (reigned 1711-1740), in an effort to pay off some of his debts, gave the estates to Count Schönborn. In this way the Rusyns lost their Hungarian landlords and came under the power of Austrian lords who sided with the emperor and who considered the Rusyns as enemies. The first thing the Austrian Baron Haber and then Count Schönborn did was to revenge themselves on the Rusyns, which was possible under existing legislation.

Although the peasant had possession of the land on which he was settled, the actual title of the property remained in the hands of the landlord. The peasant was free to use the land allocated to him as long as he and his descendants worked it. However, land left untilled was confiscated by the state. This was precisely what was done by Austrian officials who punished those Rusyns that had gone off to fight in Rákóczi's rebellion. Rusyn peasant lands on the estates of Khust-Bychkiv, Humenné, and Uzh were confiscated along with the surrounding fields, the forest, and the grazing area that were now attached to the landlord's domain. Since the wealthiest Rusyn peasants and their sons had joined Rákóczi, only the land of the poorest farmers remained intact. Some villages tried to protest against the confiscations, but to no avail. The residents of Velyki Luchky tried through all government agencies to recover their land that was given to the Schönborn estate, and they even sued. The lawsuit lasted for a century, during which time the village elders even approached Ferenc Deák,[yy] one of the greatest lawyers at the time, but he could not help

---

yy. Ferenc Deák (1803-1876) was one of the leading Hungarian political

them. According to the letter of the law, the masters of the Mukachevo estate were the Austrian counts and they had acted within their rights. Moreover, besides confiscation of lands, the Rusyns were burdened with enormous taxes which caused deep resentment.

Following the defeat of Rákóczi's rebellion, the confiscation of land was not the only reason for Rusyn poverty. The main reason was increased taxation and the arrival of Jewish usurers from Galicia. Even though the land was not returned to Rusyn peasants, their numbers steadily grew. Now 50 to 100 families had to live on land which 10 to 12 families lived on in the seventeenth century. Since it was Rákóczi's peasants that were hit hardest among the Rusyns, the so-called Highlands Action (Hegyvidéki Akció) which began in 1897 was directed at helping them first of all.

On March 7, 1897, the Greek Catholic bishop of Mukachevo, Iulii Firtsak (1836-1912, consecrated 1891), called a meeting of parliamentary deputies from Ung, Bereg, Ugocsa, and Máramaros counties to discuss a program for the improvement of the economic and cultural level of the Rusyns. The meeting dealt with these problems in great detail, among which was the question of emigration to the United States, which it determined was a result of Russian agitation and the so-called rolling ruble.[zz] The increasing emigration could be stopped only with serious measures, and memoranda were sent to all appropriate Hungarian cabinet ministers urging immediate action.

The memorandum to the Minister of Religion and Education asked for free schooling at the elementary level with concentration on farming, nursery schools, and day-care centers for children. Requests to the Minister of Trade and Commerce included the establishment of cottage industries, programs for construction of roads and regulation of rivers, and permission to import certain goods for general use. From the Minster of Internal Affairs, an end to immigration from Galicia was demanded. The memorandum to the Minister of Agriculture pointed out the necessity to reorganize grazing lands and

---

figures of the nineteenth century. Although active in the revolution of 1848, he opposed Kossuth and favored maintaining union with Austria. Two decades later, Deák was to be a key figure in bringing about the Austro-Hungarian compromise (*Ausgleich*) of 1868.

zz. The rolling ruble refers to the ostensible influx of funding from the imperial Russian government either through its embassy in Vienna or via returning Rusyn immigrants from America, which was used in pro-Orthodox and anti-Hungarian activity.

to implement other economic measures. Finally, the memorandum to the Minister of Finance requested tax exemptions for certain areas and financial credit to operate the Highlands Action.

After studying the memoranda, the Hungarian government initiated the Highlands Action in an effort to raise the economic and cultural level of the people in the Highlands as well as Transylvania. As an initial experiment, the village of Svaliava (Szolyva) in Bereg county was selected. To head the Highlands Action, the government appointed Edward Egán (1851-1901), an outstanding economist. Egán was a knowledgeable, enthusiastic, selfless, and an absolutely honest man. He carried out his task seriously and conscientiously. On March 28, 1898, he held an organizational meeting for the Highlands Action and began right away with work to assist the people and preserve their land. On February 12, Egán read a report on results of the first two years at the meeting in Mukachevo. He believed that the most important task of the Highlands Action was to give the Rusyns land. He rented 16,670 acres from the Schönborn estate, which was distributed in 41 villages among 4,303 claimants for a very low rental fee. To teach proper agricultural techniques, he established three model farms in Bereg county. In 1899, at Nyzhni Verets'ky (Alsóverecke, today Nyzhni Vorota), he conducted a six-week agricultural course for the Rusyn intelligentsia. To improve animal husbandry, 1,600 cows and 500 female sheep were brought to the area and distributed among the peasants, who were allowed to pay for them over 4 to 5 years. Five hundred workers were hired to work on road-building projects.

Credit unions were established to reorganize the area's financial structure. At the time of the report, seven credit unions existed in the Svaliava district, and all villages of that district belonged to one such credit union. During the year and a half since its establishment, the credit union voted 54,249 crowns to its 484 members. The monthly turnover of the cooperatives was around 35,000 crowns. "All we have to do," concluded Egán in his report, "is to extend the action to other districts."[74] For the location of the head office, he suggested Khust in Máramaros county and Perechyn or Velykyi Bereznyi in Ung county.

Jewish tavern owners and grocers took major steps to stop the progress of the Highlands Action. They were worried the time would come when they would no longer be able to practice usury against the village folk and that the houses and the fields of the small farmer would not be auctioned away. At the same time, anonymous elements were harassing the workers of the Highlands Action. Egán got several threatening letters saying that if he did not stop he would be eliminated. The wife of Géza Thegze, a priest in Vyshnyi Bystryi (Felsőbisztra), was attacked with a knife, and their house set on fire by unknown arsonists four times! Following such events, on September 20, 1901, Egán suddenly died. It was reported that his death was caused by an accident, although even today [1939] Rusyns believe he was a victim of revenge.

Next to Rákóczi, Egán is remembered with the greatest piety by the Rusyn people. No doubt, the death of Egán was a blow to the Highlands Action. Nevertheless, the government continued and even enlarged the program. Ten years after Egán's death, that is, in 1911, the Minister of Agriculture reported on the progress of the Highlands Action. According to this report, since the beginning of the program 29,000 acres of land were given in 1½ x 6 acre lots to 3,063 peasants in 66 villages from land rented from estate owners by the government and leased to peasants for a very low rent. In addition to this, 8,400 acres were given in perpetual ownership to individual peasants and communities.

To stop loan abuses and to reduce usury, more credit unions and cooperatives with storage facilities were founded. The former offered loans on easy terms; the latter, healthy competition. Both measures were effective weapons against both types of usury. By 1911, 148 credit unions had 35,819 members with shares amounting to 2,577,580 crowns. Loans to members totalled over 6 million crowns, and the gross income of the cooperative storage facilities was in 1909 already 1,863,245 crowns.

In order to prevent ignorant people from falling into hands of speculators and criminals, free legal advice was given. The government gave peasants legal advice on questions out of court as well as during court proceedings.

To improve animal husbandry, many important measures were undertaken. Breeding stock was made available at greatly reduced prices. Because a basic factor in animal husbandry is adequate grazing facilities and hay growing, measures were taken to improve both these aspects. Thus, the livestock of the people had better grass in the summer and better hay in stables during the winter.

To change backward farming practices, model farms were created with the intention to show by example that better practices would result in greater income. To disseminate agricultural knowledge, a dairy school was opened at the Royal Hungarian Highland Farming Station in Nyzhni Verets'ky. Twenty-four students from the Carpathians were able to study there free, with all expenses paid by the state, and with complete training in practices such as milk-handling, cheese-making, and butter-churning. During winter months, evening courses were offered in various villages. All these efforts led to the abandonment of antiquated farming methods and to the adoption of modern techniques. To assure the success of the new methods, improved seed was sold at low prices and farm machinery was made available at reduced prices.

In order to enhance the population's earning power, employment offices were opened. Year after year jobs were found for between 7,000 and 8,000 workers from the highlands on the Great Hungarian Plain. Their total income was between 400,000 and 500,000 crowns. New sources of income were created as well, and cottage industries were encouraged to make profitable use of the long winter months. Cooperatives embracing all kinds of cottage industries provided 3,400 peasants with work and extra earning power. However, World War I and the Czech occupation that followed put an end to the Highlands Action. Therefore, today [i.e. 1939], the Hungarian government and Subcarpathian society have a lot of work ahead of them.

Statistical Appendix

Rusyns live in [Hungary's] Subcarpathia and in smaller numbers in the counties of Zemplén, Sáros and Szepes in Slovakia.[aaa] According to decree no. 6200, dated 1939, the Hungarian government divided Máramaros, Bereg, Ugocsa, and Ung counties, that is, the areas in Subcarpathia where Rusyns form the majority of the population, into three administrative units: Bereg, Máramaros, and Ung. At the head of Subcarpathian territory as a whole is a commissioner appointed by

---

aaa. The discussion in this appendix deals primarily with the former Czechoslovak province of Subcarpathian Rus' (Podkarpatská Rus) that was in two stages reincorporated into Hungary: (1) on November 2, 1938, the Vienna Award granted Hungary the southern, primarily Magyar-inhabited areas of the province, including the cities of Uzhhorod, Mukachevo, and Berehovo; (2) on March 15, 1939, when Hitler destroyed what remained of the post-Munich Czechoslovak republic, Hungarian troops entered the rest of Subcarpathian Rus' (by then known as Carpatho-Ukraine) and annexed it to Hungary, where it remained until the arrival of the Soviet Red Army in September 1944. During the early months of its rule in Subcarpathian Rus', which lasted from 1939 to 1944, Hungary made promises to grant the region limited autonomy, but this was never implemented.

the head of the Hungarian state. The commissioner exercises the right to issue decrees, a right usually belonging to county councils, and he has all the administrative authority of the lord-lieutenant [in Hungarian counties].

With regard to questions that concern the Subcarpathian territory as a whole, the commissioner is informed by a state-appointed advisor. To deal with these problems, the Prime Minister of Hungary appoints a judicial and advisory council to assist the commissioner. The council has eight members. The official languages in the Subcarpathian territory are Hungarian and Rusyn. Those state decrees which concern the Subcarpathian territory are published by the commissioner in parallel Rusyn and Hungarian texts in the official organ of Subcarpathia, *Podkarpatskii vîstnyk*, at the same time they appear in the official *Budapesti közlöny*. The *Podkarpatskii vîstnyk* also publishes ordinances issued by the commissioner and all other official documents that pertain to Subcarpathia. With a few exceptions, the organization of city and village administrations are the same as in the rest of Hungary.

According to Lajos Thirring's study, the preliminary census of Subcarpathia, carried out in July 1939, indicated that the size of the territory was 12,146 km^2 and its population—671,962 inhabitants.[75] The distribution of the population according to administrative territories and districts is as follows:

Administrative unit and district	Total civilian population		Annual growth of population (in percentages)
	1910	July 15, 1939	
A) Bereg			
Irshava district	42,528	56,770	1.17
Mukachevo and vicinity district	52,052	73,379	1.29
Svaliava district	43,403	60,930	1.42
Subtotal	138,883	190,079	1.29
B) Máramaros			
Khust district	54,584	81,395	1.72
Sevliush district	44,533	61,719	1.35
Mizhhir''ia district	31,682	41,458	1.08
Rakhiv district	50,782	67,874	1.18
Tiachiv district	64,364	94,137	1.62
Subtotal	245,945	346,583	1.44
C) Ung			
Velykyi Berezhnyi district	42,128	52,004	0.82
Perechyn district	21,290	26,279	0.82
Sobrance district	22,472	24,243	0.28
Uzhhorod and vicinity district	21,054	25,638	0.76
Subtotal	106,944	128,164	0.70
Total for all Subcarpathian territory	491,772	664,826	1.24
D) Villages and partial townships in the returned Highland area	4,671	7,136	0.85
Total	496,443	671,962	1.24

Data referring to the mother-tongue and religion of the population were not yet evaluated [at the time the book was written], but it can be seen from the results so far that about 65 to 70 percent of the population is Rusyn, the balance Magyar, Jewish (from Poland), and German.

In addition to Subcarpathia, there are [in Slovakia] about 100,000 Rusyns living in the counties Zemplén, Sáros, and Szepes. Also, on the left bank of the Tysa, in that area which the peace Treaty of Trianon gave to Romania, there are about 20,000 Rusyns.

The Subcarpathian Territory (Kárpátalja vajdaság)

On July 23, 1940, the Royal Hungarian Government submitted to its parliament a proposal to establish a Subcarpathian Territory. In effect, this was intended to legalize (apart from one or two insignificant differences) Ministerial Decree No. 6200 (1939) and the *de facto* administrative situation that already existed in Subcarpathia. Faithful to the thousand-year-old principles of a policy that is in the spirit of St. Stephen, the new law will assure that Rusyns can sustain and foster their customs, language, and culture in their homes, schools, and churches.

The implementation of the Subcarpathian Territory does not create a state within a state and does not destroy the unity of Hungary. The public administration of the Subcarpathian Territory is identical with that of the country as a whole. There is only one difference: judicial and administrative matters are dealt with in two languages—Hungarian and Rusyn. The new act of parliament also establishes in regions of mixed population complete and real equality before the law.

Author's Notes

1. Károly Tagányi, "Gyepü és gyepüelve," *Magyar nyelv,* IX, 3, 4, 5, 6 (Budapest, 1913), pp. 97-104, 145-152, 201-206, 254-266.

2. Władysław Semkowicz, "Geograficzne podstawy Polski Chrobrego," *Kwartalnik Historyczny,* XXXIX, 2 (L'viv, 1925), pp. 258-314; Karol Potkański, "Kraków przed Piastami," *Rozprawy Polskiej Akademii Umiejętnosci,* XXXV: *Wydział Historyczno-filozoficzny,* Serya II, tom X (Cracow, 1898), pp. 101-255; Tadeusz Zachorowski, "Węgierskie i polskie osadnictwo Spiżu do połowy XIV w.," *ibid.,* LII, Serya II, tom XXVII (1909), pp. 191-283; Stanislaw Arnold, "Terytorja plemienne Polski Piastowskej," in *Prace komitetu dla atlasu historycznego Polski,* Vol. II (Cracow, 1927).

3. Alexander Bonkáló, "Die ungarländischen Ruthenen," *Ungarische Jahrbücher,* I (Berlin, 1922), pp. 221-226; Antal Hodinka, *A munkácsi görögkatholikus püspőkség tőrténete* (Budapest, 1910).

4. Anonymi, "Gesta Hungarorum," section 10, in Emericus Szentpétery, ed., *Scriptores rerum Hungarorum,* Vol. I (Budapest, 1937), p. 47.

5. Anonymi, "Gesta Hungarorum," section 57, in *ibid.,* p. 113.

6. Hermann J. Bidermann, *Die ungarischen Ruthenen, ihr Wohngebiet, ihr Erwerb, und ihre Geschichte,* Vol. II (Innsbruck, 1867), p. 44.

7. Vasilii O. Kliuchevskii, *Kurs russkoi istorii,* Vol. I (Moscow, 1904), pp. 358-359.

8. M. Istvánffy, *Historiarum de rebus Hungaricis libri XXXIV* (Vienna, 1758), p. 168.

9. Hodinka, *A munkácsi,* p. 21.

10. Tivadar Lehoczky, "Adalékok a kenézek intézményéhez," *Történelmi könyvtár,* XIII (Budapest, 1890).

11. Hodinka, *A munkácsi,* p. 72.

12. Antal Hodinka, ed., *Az orosz evkönyvek magyar vonatkozásai* (Budapest, 1916), pp. 359 and 349.

13. From the entry for the year 1226, drawn from the translation of George A. Perfecky, *The Galician Volynian Chronicle* (Munich, 1973), p. 31.

14. Iul'ian A. Iavorskii, "Staraia latinskaia zapiska o s. Guklivoi," *Karpatskii sviet*, II, 10 (Uzhhorod, 1929), p. 739.

15. Kőszeghy, "Lipcsey Zsigmond orosz telepesei Máramarosban," *Magyar gazdaságtörténeti szemle*, I (Budapest, 1894), pp. 331-343.

16. Bonkáló provided no specific source for this quotation—editor.

17. Antal Hodinka, *Rákóczi Ferenc fejedelem és a 'gens fidelissima'* (Pécs, 1937), p. 3.

18. *Ibid.*, p. 55.

19. From a report by the Royal Court Chancery, dated September 17, 1751. See H. Bidermann, *Russiche Umtriebe in Ungarn* (Innsbruck, 1867).

20. Bonkáló provided no specific source for this quotation—editor.

21. Sándor Bonkáló, *A kárpátalji rutén irodalom és művelődes* (Pécs, 1935), pp. 42-43.

22. For a detailed description of Szabó's reports, see Gábor Darás, *A Ruténföld elszakításának előzményei, 1890-1920* (Ujpest, 1936), pp. 64-83.

23. *Ibid.*, p. 99.

24. Aleksei L. Petrov, *Drevnieishiia gramoty po istorii karpato-russkoi tserkvi i ierarkhii, 1391-1498 g.* (Prague, 1930). In this work, Petrov summarizes the preliminary results of his research and published a bibliography of the problem.

25. *Ibid.*, pp. xi-xii.

26. Joannicis Basilovits, *Brevis notitia Fundationis Theodori Koriathovits*, Vol. I, pts. 1-2 (Košice, 1799).

27. Harry Bresslau, *Handbuch der Urkundenlehre für Deutschland und Italien*, 2 vols. (Leipzig, 1912-15).

28. Bonkáló provided no specific source for this quotation—editor.

29. Bonkáló provided no specific source for this quotation—editor.

30. Bidermann, *Die ungarischen Ruthenen*, Vol. II, p. 59.

31. Bonkáló provided no specific source for this quotation—editor.

32. Bonkáló provided no specific source for this quotation—editor.

33. Bonkáló provided no sources for these quotations—editor.

34. Bonkáló provided no source for this quotation, which is probably drawn from Károly Mészáros, *A magyarországi oroszok története* (Budapest, 1850). Among the confusing aspects of the Mészaros account is the reference to Dózsa, the only one known in Transylvania history being György Dózsa who two centuries later led a peasant uprising in 1512—editor.

35. Bonkáló provided no source for this quotation—editor.

36. *Slovo*, XIV, 69 (L'viv, 1874).

37. Stepan Tomashivs'kyi, "Etnografichna karta Uhors'koî Rusy," in V. I. Lamanskii, ed., *Stat'i po slavianoviedieniiu*, Vol. III (St. Petersburg, 1910), p. 201, note 7.

38. The English translation is taken from Samuel Cross and Olgerd P. Sherbowitz-Wetzor, eds., *The Russian Primary Chronicle: Laurentian Text* (Cambridge, Mass., 1973), p. 59.

39. A. Krymskii, *Ukrainskaia grammatika*, Vol. I (Moscow, 1907), pp. 128-129, 139-191.

40. Josef Lad. Pič, "Rodovy být na Slovensku a v Uherské Rusi," *Časopis Musea království českého*, LII (Prague, 1878), pp. 189-199 and 344-354.

41. Bonkáló provided no specific source for this quotation—editor.

42. Bonkáló provided no sources for these quotations—editor.

43. For a more detailed discussion, see S. Czambel, *Slovenská reč a jej miesto v rodine slovanských jazykov*, Vol. I (Turčiansky Sv. Martin, 1906).

44. The information in this chapter is based on Bonkáló, *A kárpátalji rutén irodalom*.

45. Bonkáló provided no specific source for this quotation—editor.

46. Bonkáló provided no source for this quotation—editor.

47. A. L. Petrov, *Drevnieishaia tserkovnoslavianskaia gramota 1404 g. o karpatorusskoi territorii* (Uzhhorod, 1927).

48. I. A. Iavorskii, *Vetkhozavietnyia bibleiskiia skazaniia v tserkovno-uchitel'noi obrabotkie kontsa XVII v.* (Uzhhorod and Prague, 1927), p. 58.

49. *Ibid.*, pp. 28, 35, 36, 49, 58, 66, 68.

50. *Ibid.*, p. 6.

51. O. Broch, *Slavische Phonetik* (Heidelberg, 1911), pp. 49, 80.

52. Bonkáló provided no specific source for this quotation—editor.

53. Bonkáló provided no specific page number source for this quotation—editor.

54. The English translation of this poem, "Podkarpatskî rusyny," (Subcarpathian Rusyns), is by Paul R. Magocsi, in his "Carpatho-Rusyn Language and Literature," *Carpatho-Rusyn American*, III, 4 (Fairview, N.J., 1980), p. 4—editor.

55. From the poem entitled "Vruchanie" (Dedication), translation by Magocsi, in *ibid.*—editor.

56. Bonkáló provided no specific bibliographical data for this quotation—editor.

57. Bonkáló provided no specific bibliographical data for this quotation—editor.

58. *Listok*, XIX, 22 (Uzhhorod, 1903).

59. Bonkáló stated the 1248 document comes from the *Codex Arpadi cont. Szentpétery Scriptores rerum Hungarorum*, Vol. VII, doc. 183, and p. 263. He did not indicate, however, in what specific work Dobrians'kyi cited the document—editor.

60. Bonkáló provided no source for this quotation—editor.

61. Bonkáló provided no specific page number sources for the quotations in this paragraph—editor.

62. Cited in *Russkii narodnyi golos* (Uzhhorod, 1938), No. 71.

63. Bonkáló provided no specific source for this quotation—editor.

64. *Görög katholikus szemle* (Uzhhorod), March 25, 1900.

65. Among these were collections by Volodymyr Hnatiuk (1897-1900), Iakiv Holovats'kyi (1878), Grigorii Devollan (1885), Ivan Verkhrats'kyi (1899-1902), and Mykhal Vrabel' (1890).

66. Bonkáló provided no source for this quotation—editor.

67. Bonkáló provided no specific source for this quotation—editor.

68. Bonkáló provided no source for this quotation—editor.

69. Ignác Acsádi, *A magyar jobbágyság története* (Budapest, 1906).

70. Bonkáló provided no specific source for this quotation—editor.

71. Bonkáló provided no specific source for this quotation—editor.

72. František Gabriel, "Poddanské poměry na užhorodském panstvi ke konci XVIII stoleti," *Naukovyi zbornyk 'Tovarystva Prosvita'*, X (Uzhhorod, 1934).

73. Bonkáló provided no specific source for this quotation—editor.

74. Bonkáló provided no specific source for this quotation—editor.

75. Lajos Thirring, "A visszatért Kárpátaljai területen végrehajtott népösszeirás előzetes eredményei," *Magyar statisztikai szemle*, XVII, 8 (Budapest, 1939).

Bibliography

Many articles and books were published about the Rusyns since the outset of the last century. Initially, much was written in the Russian Empire. In the beginning of the nineteenth century, Vladimir B. Bronevskii, G.A. Glinka, Petr I. Keppen, Nikolai I. Nadezhdin, Ivan S. Orlaj, and Izmail I. Sreznevskii among others informed the Russian public about the Rusyns of Subcarpathia. The Hungarian public learned about the Rusyns from the books of Antal Décsy (1797) and Károly Mészáros (1850) and from articles which were published in the *Tudományos Gyűjtemény* and other journals. However, these works published in the first half of the nineteenth century have no scholarly value.

The first scholarly work about Rusyns was written by Hermann Bidermann, and serious historical research began only after the publication of his [two-volume] work (1862-67). Besides Hungarian historians, only the Russians Nikolai P. Barsov, Anton S. Budilovich, Vladimir A. Frantsev, Ivan Filevich, Iakov K. Grot, Dimitrii I. Ilovaiskii, Arist A. Kunik, Aleksei L. Petrov, Aleksei A. Shakhmatov, Aleksei I. Sobolevskii, and Vasilii G. Vasilevskii took part. It is worth mentioning that among the Ukrainians, Mykhailo Hrushevs'kyi, Ivan Franko, Stepan Tomashivs'kyi; among the Slovaks, Samo Czambel and G. Mišik; and among the Czechs, Václav Chaloupecký, Karel Kadlec, and Lubor Niederle wrote about the Rusyns. As for Rusyn historians, Nikolai Beskyd, Iosyf Kamins'kyi, Irynei Kondratovych, and Sulynchak used hardly any documentary sources. There is, however, much valuable material in [Rusyn] journals and newspapers.

Literature [dealing with Rusyns] from the nineteenth century is discussed by Vladimir A. Frantsev in his "Obzor vazhnieishikh izuchenii Ugorskoi Rusi" (1901), with additional material and corrections to Frantsev's work in Volodymyr Hnatiuk's review in the

Zapysky Naukovoho tovarystva im. Shevchenka, XLV, 1 (L'iviv, 1902), pp. 41-46.

Other bibliographical works include two volumes by Jiří Král, *Geografická bibliografie Podkarpatské Rusi*, pts. 1 and 2 *za roky 1923-1926* (Prague 1923-28), with the comments and additions to those volumes by Florian Zapletal, *Kralová bibliografie Podkarpatské Rusi* (Olomouc, 1925), and the earlier historiographical survey by Evhenii Perfets'kyi [Perfetskii], "Obzor ugro-russkoi istoriografii," *Izvestiia Otdieleniia russkago iazyka i slovesnosti Imperatorskoi akademii nauk*, XIX, 1 (St. Petersburg, 1914).

Works of greater importance

Bidermann, Hermann J. *Die ungarischen Ruthenen, ihr Wohngebiet, ihr Erwerb, und ihre Geschichte*. 2 vols. Innsbruck, 1862-67.

Bonkáló, Sándor. *A kárpátalji rután irodalom és művelődes*. Pécs, 1935.

──────. *A magyar rutének*. Budapest, 1920.

──────. "Die ungarländischen Ruthenen." *Ungarische Jahrbücher*, I (Berlin, 1922), pp. 215-232, 313-341.

Czambel, Samo. *Slovenská reč a jej miesto v rodine slovanských jazykov*, Vol. I. Turčiansky Sv. Martin, 1906.

Darás, Gábor. *A Ruténföld elszakításának előzményei (1890-1920)*. Ujpest, 1936.

Hodinka, Antal. *A kárpátalji rutének lakóhelye gazdaságuk és multjuk*. Budapest, 1923.

──────. *A munkácsi görög-katholikus püspökség története*. Budapest, 1910.

──────, ed. *A munkácsi görög-szertartású püspökség okmánytára*, Vol. I: *1458-1715*. Uzhhorod, 1911.

Niederle, Lubor. *Slovanské starožitnosti: původ a počatky Slovanů východných*. Prague, 1924.

Petrov, Aleksei L. *Drevnieishiia gramoty po istorii karpato-russkoi tserkvi i ierarkhii, 1391-1498 g.* Prague, 1930.

──────. "Kanonicheskaia vizitatsiia 1750-1767 gg. v varmediakh Zemplinskoi, Sharishskoi, Shpishskoi i Abauiskoi." *Naukovyi zbornyk Tovarystva 'Prosvîta'*, III (Uzhhorod, 1924), pp. 104-135.

──────. *Materiialy po istorii Zakarpatskoi (b. Ugorskoi) Rusi*, 8 vols. St. Petersburg, 1906-14 and Prague, 1923.

Much interesting material can be found in Hungarian scholarly journals; in the *Naukovŷi zbôrnyk Tovarystva 'Prosvîta'*, 14 vols. (Uzhhorod, 1922-38); and in the more popular monthly journal of regional history and culture, *Podkarpatska Rus'* (Uzhhorod, 1924-36), especially the studies of Vasylii Hadzhega and František Gabriel.

Index